PRENTICE HALL

UNITED STATES HISTORY

RECONSTRUCTION TO THE PRESENT

CURRICULUM

Reading and Note Taking Study Guide

PEARSON

Prentice
Hall

Upper Saddle River, New Jersey
Boston, Massachusetts

PEARSON

Prentice
Hall

Upper Saddle River, New Jersey
Boston, Massachusetts

ISBN 0-13-202584-1

1 2 3 4 5 6 7 8 9 10   10 09 08 07 06

Contents

How to Use This Book

The **Reading and Note Taking Study Guide** will help you better understand the content of *Prentice Hall United States History*. This book will also develop your reading, vocabulary, and note taking skills. Each study guide consists of two components. The first component focuses on developing the graphic organizers that appear in your textbook.

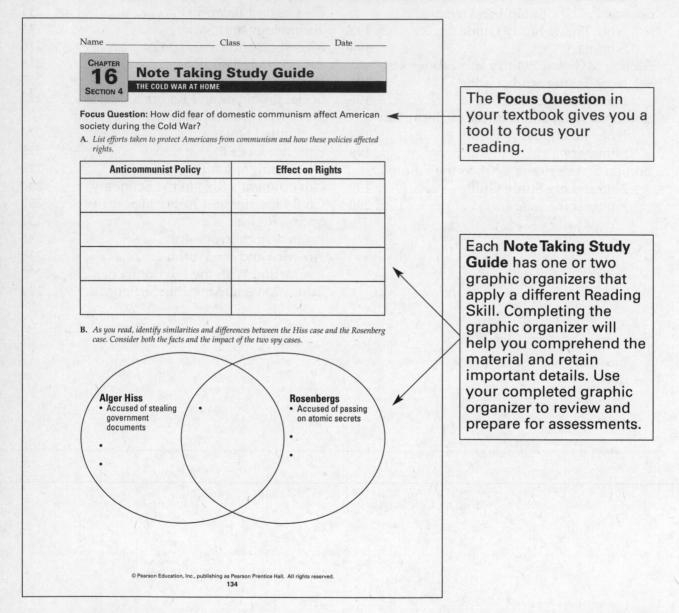

Name _____ Class _____ Date _____

CHAPTER 16 SECTION 4

Note Taking Study Guide

THE COLD WAR AT HOME

Focus Question: How did fear of domestic communism affect American society during the Cold War?

A. *List efforts taken to protect Americans from communism and how these policies affected rights.*

Anticommunist Policy	Effect on Rights

B. *As you read, identify similarities and differences between the Hiss case and the Rosenberg case. Consider both the facts and the impact of the two spy cases.*

Alger Hiss
- Accused of stealing government documents
- •
- •

Rosenbergs
- Accused of passing on atomic secrets
- •
- •

134

The **Focus Question** in your textbook gives you a tool to focus your reading.

Each **Note Taking Study Guide** has one or two graphic organizers that apply a different Reading Skill. Completing the graphic organizer will help you comprehend the material and retain important details. Use your completed graphic organizer to review and prepare for assessments.

The second component highlights the central themes, issues, and concepts of each section.

CHAPTER 16
SECTION 4

Section Summary

THE COLD WAR AT HOME

The **Red Scare**—public fear that communists were working to destroy America both from within and without—spurred President Truman in 1947 to investigate federal employees. About 3,000 people were dismissed or resigned. The Truman administration also used the 1940 **Smith Act**, a law against advocating violent overthrow of the government, to send 11 U.S. Communist Party members to prison. Meanwhile, the House Committee on Un-American Activities (HUAC) investigated subversive activities throughout American life, including academic institutions, labor unions, and city halls. In 1947, HUAC targeted the **Hollywood Ten**, a group of left-wing writers, directors, and producers. They refused to testify against themselves but were sent to prison. Movie executives then circulated a **blacklist** that named entertainment figures suspected of communist ties, shattering many careers.

Two sensational spy trials increased the country's suspicion of communists. The first one concerned **Alger Hiss**, a government employee who had helped organize the United Nations. In 1948, Whittaker Chambers, a former member of the Communist Party and an espionage agent, named Hiss as one of his government contacts. Hiss denied everything before HUAC but was sentenced to five years in prison. The second trial involved **Julius and Ethel Rosenberg**, who were accused of passing secret information about nuclear science to Soviet agents. The Rosenbergs claimed that they were being persecuted because they were Jewish and held unpopular beliefs. They were convicted in a highly controversial trial and executed in 1953.

Joseph R. McCarthy, a senator from Wisconsin, also fanned Americans' fears. He claimed he had a long list of communists in the State Department, but each time he was asked to give specific names and numbers, his figures changed. Still, with the outbreak of the Korean War in 1950, McCarthy's popularity soared. **McCarthyism** became a catchword for the senator's vicious style of reckless charges. McCarthy's targets grew bigger, and in 1954, he went after the United States Army. After viewers saw him badger witnesses and twist the truth during televised hearings, he lost his strongest supporters. The end of the Korean War in 1953 and McCarthy's downfall in 1954 signaled the decline of the Red Scare.

Review Questions

1. How were the Smith Act and HUAC supposed to discourage communism in the United States?

   _____

   _____

2. What events led to the decline of the Red Scare?

   _____

   _____

135

READING CHECK

What happened to the Hollywood Ten?

_____

_____

_____

VOCABULARY STRATEGY

What does the word *academic* mean in the underlined sentence? Use context clues and your prior knowledge to help you figure out what *academic* means.

_____

_____

_____

READING SKILL

Identify Causes and Effects
Discuss the events that led to McCarthyism and the popularity of the senator from Wisconsin.

_____

_____

_____

Each **Summary** highlights **Terms, People, and Places** in boldface, and summarizes the key points in the section.

The **Reading Check** will help you recall, identify, or define important facts.

The **Vocabulary Strategy** provides methods for increasing word recognition and comprehension of high-level vocabulary.

The **Reading Skill** question provides an opportunity to apply the reading skill introduced in your textbook.

The **Review Questions** help you to review content and assess your understanding of the section.

The **American Issues Study Guide** supports the **American Issues Connector** features found in your text. These worksheets will help you track key issues that Americans have debated throughout their history. Each worksheet covers one of the 21 recurring American issues over time.

Name _____ Class _____ Date _____

American Issues Study Guide

Civil Liberties and National Security

Enduring Question: What is the proper balance between national security and civil liberties?

Record information about the events listed below, as you study them in your textbook.
- *Describe the situation that brought the issue into discussion.*
- *Identify the arguments at the time on both sides of the issue. Discuss the arguments for limiting civil liberties. Discuss the arguments against limiting civil liberties.*
- *Indicate how the issue was resolved at the time. Did the situation change? If so, how?*

1790s: Undeclared War With France (See chapter "The Nation's Beginnings")

_____
_____
_____
_____
_____

1860s: Civil War (See chapter "Crisis, Civil War, and Reconstruction")

_____
_____
_____
_____
_____

1940s: World War II (See chapter "World War II")

_____
_____
_____
_____
_____
_____

232

The **Enduring Question** helps you think about the impact of the concept throughout history.

The three-step process in the direction lines will help you to structure your answer.

Use the chapter references following each item to locate relevant information in your textbook.

CHAPTER 1
SECTION 1

Note Taking Study Guide

MANY CULTURES MEET

Focus Question: What were the causes and effects of European arrival in the Americas?

Identify the causes and effects of European arrival in the Americas.

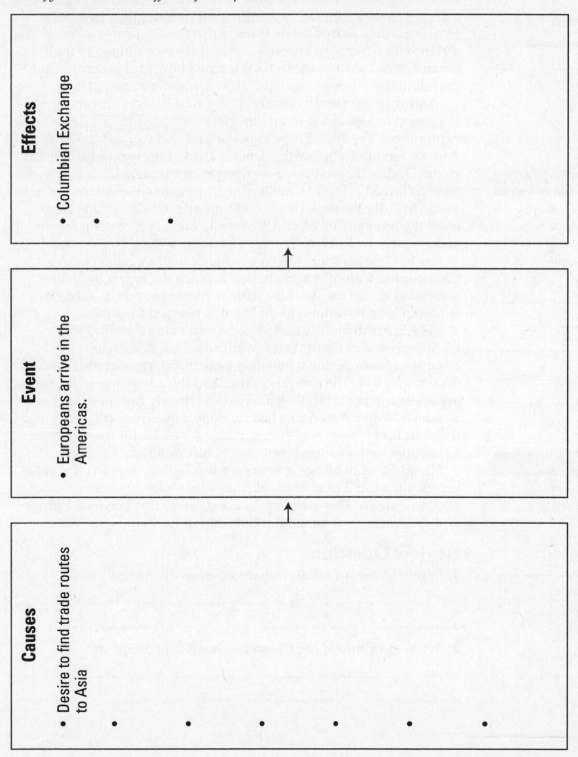

Effects
- Columbian Exchange
-
-

Event
- Europeans arrive in the Americas.

Causes
- Desire to find trade routes to Asia
- • • • • • •

CHAPTER 1

SECTION 1

Section Summary

MANY CULTURES MEET

READING CHECK

What were Spanish invaders known as?

_____

_____

_____

VOCABULARY STRATEGY

What does the word *diverse* mean in the underlined sentence? Look for context clues in the surrounding words and phrases.

_____

_____

_____

READING SKILL

Identify Causes and Effects What were the effects of the Middle Passage?

_____

_____

_____

Most scientists believe that the first inhabitants of the Americas came from northeastern Asia between 15,000 and 40,000 years ago. Over the generations, the American Indians expanded southward, filling the continents of North and South America. They developed diverse cultures as they adapted to the different climates they inhabited. However, they shared many traits. An extended family evolved into a **clan** with a common ancestor. Several clans combined to make up a **band** of Indians. As the Indians learned how to grow crops, the population grew, leading to the growth of towns and cities.

During the fifteenth century, scientific advances and an increase in economic wealth led some Europeans to sponsor voyages of exploration. The Portuguese took the lead and reached the West African kingdoms below the Sahara. There, they expanded the slave trade. During the next three centuries, slave traders from European nations forced at least 11 million Africans across the Atlantic. Known as the **Middle Passage,** this brutal transatlantic slave trade weakened the economy of West Africa while making European merchants and empires wealthy.

In 1492, Spain sponsored a voyage headed by Italian mariner **Christopher Columbus.** He hoped to reach the Indies by sailing westward across the Atlantic. After exploring several Caribbean islands, Columbus thought that he had reached the Indies.

The Spanish rapidly conquered a vast empire around the Caribbean and in Central and South America. Known as **conquistadores,** Spanish invaders were brave, resourceful, ruthless, and destructive. The conquistadores had the advantage of horses and steel weapons, but they also carried deadly European diseases to which Native Americans had no immunity. These plagues killed thousands of Native Americans, making it easier for the Europeans to conquer and colonize North and South America.

In addition to bringing new people into the Americas, the colonizers introduced new animals. They also took American products back to Europe. This exchange of goods and ideas between Europe and the Americas is called the **Columbian Exchange.**

Review Questions

1. Why did the American Indians develop diverse cultures?

_____

_____

2. What did Christopher Columbus hope to accomplish?

_____

_____

Name _____ Class _____ Date _____

Focus Question: What important ideas and major events led to the American Revolution?

Note the sequence of events that led to the American Revolution by making a series-of-events chain.

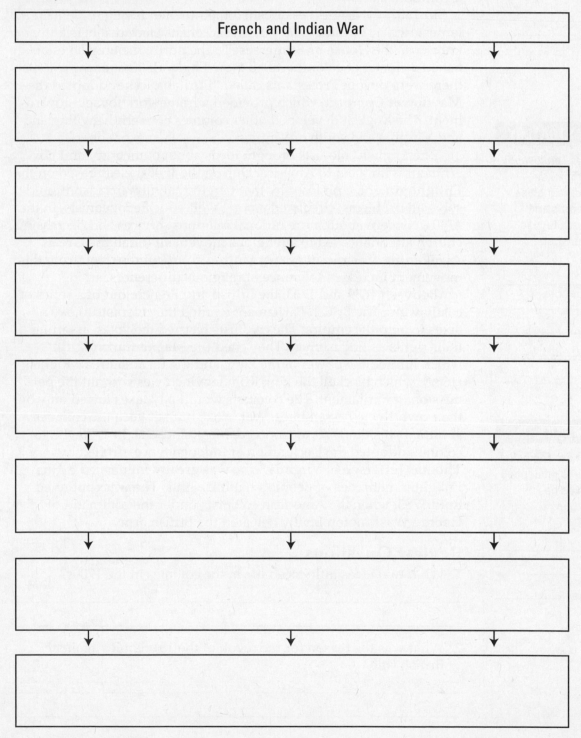

French and Indian War

CHAPTER 1 SECTION 2

Section Summary
THE AMERICAN REVOLUTION

READING CHECK

What was the Great Awakening?

_____

_____

_____

VOCABULARY STRATEGY

What does the word *philosophy* mean in the underlined sentence? Look for context clues in the surrounding words and phrases. Use this strategy to help you figure out what *philosophy* means.

_____

_____

_____

READING SKILL

Recognize Sequence The belief in what type of rights influenced Thomas Jefferson as he wrote the Declaration of Independence?

_____

_____

Spain established colonies in the present-day Southwest and Florida, where forts called presidios were set up for protection and missions were set up to convert Native Americans to Christianity. The French established colonies in Canada and along the Mississippi River valley in Louisiana.

In 1607, the English established their first enduring settlement at Jamestown in Virginia. The Virginia colonists elected a legislature known as the **House of Burgesses.** To the north, the English established a cluster of colonies called New England. Most of the colonists there were devout Protestants called "Puritans." They adopted the **Mayflower Compact,** which provided a framework for self-government. The English developed other colonies between New England and Virginia and south of Virginia.

The English colonists brought ideas about democracy and government with them to America. During the 1700s, ideas based on the **Enlightenment,** a philosophy that taught that human reason could solve all problems, circulated among well-educated colonists. In the 1740s, concern about more rational religious services and decreasing church attendance led to a religious movement called the **Great Awakening.** The rise of new organized churches resulting from this movement increased tolerance of religious differences.

Between 1689 and 1763, the British and French fought a series of costly wars. The British Parliament wanted the colonists to pay new taxes to help the empire. The colonists resisted the taxes, asserting their rights as Englishmen. They cited the **Magna Carta** (1215), which limited the power of the king, and the English Bill of Rights (1689), which blocked the king from levying taxes without the permission of Parliament. The colonists would pay taxes levied only by their own elected assemblies. War broke out between the colonies and the British in 1775, at Concord, Massachusetts. In 1776, the 13 colonies adopted the Declaration of Independence, drafted by **Thomas Jefferson** of Virginia, who was greatly influenced by the Enlightenment idea of people's natural rights. The war continued until 1783, when the American colonists under the command of **George Washington** finally defeated the British army.

Review Questions

1. What two ideas influenced life in the colonies in the 1700s?

_____

_____

2. What was the reason for the revolt of the 13 colonies against British rule?

_____

_____

CHAPTER 1
SECTION 3

Note Taking Study Guide
THE CONSTITUTION

Focus Question: What ideas and debates led to the Constitution and Bill of Rights?

A. *Complete the timeline below with important dates that led to the formation of the U.S. government.*

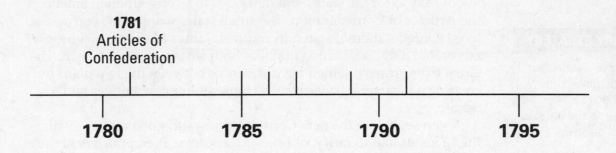

1781
Articles of
Confederation

1780   1785   1790   1795

B. *As you read, identify similarities and differences between the Federalists and the Antifederalists.*

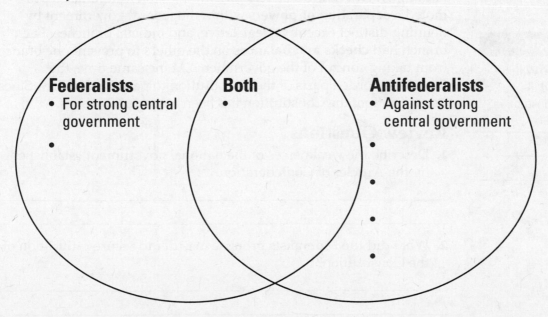

Federalists
• For strong central
  government
•

Both
•

Antifederalists
• Against strong
  central government
•
•
•
•

Name _____ Class _____ Date _____

<table>
<tr><td>CHAPTER
1
SECTION 3</td><td>**Section Summary**
THE CONSTITUTION</td></tr>
</table>

READING CHECK

What is federalism?

_____

_____

_____

After winning their independence from Britain, the former American colonies became states. Each state created a constitution and established a government. Most of these state constitutions included a **bill of rights,** a list of freedoms guaranteed by the state government.

In 1781, the 13 states adopted their first federal constitution. Under the Articles of Confederation, most power remained with the states. Without the ability to levy taxes, the federal government could not pay its immense war debt. Similarly, the weak confederation could not defend American interests on the frontier. <u>The Spanish in Louisiana tried to constrain western American settlements by closing the port of New Orleans.</u>

In May 1787, the states sent delegates to a convention to amend the Articles of Confederation. The small states wanted to keep a loose confederation of states. In contrast, **James Madison** of Virginia advocated a national union that was both strong and republican. The Great Compromise settled the differences between the two plans by creating a bicameral legislature: a House of Representatives and a Senate.

Even so, before the new Constitution would go into effect, 9 of the 13 states had to **ratify,** or officially approve, it. Supporters of the Constitution, known as Federalists, wanted the United States to have a strong central government. Opponents, known as Antifederalists, objected to the Constitution because they thought it gave the national government far too much power. Because the most powerful argument of the Antifederalists was that the proposed Constitution lacked a bill of rights, the Federalists promised to add a bill of rights. In 1789, states ratified the federal Bill of Rights.

The Constitution divided power between the states and the nation, which is known as **federalism.** The Constitution also promoted a **separation of powers** within the federal government by defining distinct executive, legislative, and judicial branches. Each branch had **checks and balances** on the others to prevent one branch from taking control of the government. At the same time, the founders worded parts of the Constitution to permit flexibility. Since its ratification, the Constitution has been amended 27 times.

VOCABULARY STRATEGY

What does the word *constrain* mean in the underlined sentence? Use context clues in the surrounding words and phrases to figure out the meaning of *constrain*.

_____

_____

_____

READING SKILL

Recognize Sequence Which constitution preceded the current United States Constitution?

_____

_____

_____

Review Questions

1. Describe the weaknesses of the national government established by the Articles of Confederation.

_____

_____

2. What did the Federalists promise in order to secure ratification of the Constitution?

_____

_____

Name _____ Class _____ Date _____

Focus Question: How did the United States and its government change in the late 1700s and early 1800s?

List the major accomplishments of each President in the chart below.

President	Accomplishments
George Washington	• • • •
John Adams	• •
	• • • • • • •
	•
	•

Name _____ Class _____ Date _____

Section Summary
THE NEW REPUBLIC

READING CHECK

What was the Sedition Act?

_____

_____

_____

VOCABULARY STRATEGY

What does the word *compensating* mean in the underlined sentence? Look for context clues in the surrounding words, phrases, and sentences. Circle the word below that is a synonym for *compensating*.

• paying

• depriving

READING SKILL

Categorize List at least two actions the United States took to avoid war.

_____

_____

_____

After the Revolutionary War, Secretary of the Treasury Alexander Hamilton used the clause of the Constitution allowing Congress to enact laws for the "general welfare," to create a financial plan to pay off the war debt. <u>Critics from the South said that it favored merchants from the Northeast by compensating them with tax dollars.</u>

The French Revolution in 1789 started a war between Britain and France. The United States declared its neutrality but continued to trade with Britain and France. The British navy then began seizing U.S. merchant ships trading with French colonies. To avoid war, John Jay negotiated Jay's Treaty between Britain and the United States. Congress then passed the Alien and Sedition acts in 1798. The **Alien Act** made it more difficult for immigrants to become citizens. The **Sedition Act** made it a crime for citizens to publicly discredit the federal government.

Thomas Jefferson was elected President in 1800. In 1803, the Supreme Court decision of *Marbury* v. *Madison* asserted **judicial review,** the power to review the constitutionality of a federal law. Also in 1803, Jefferson bought a vast territory extending from the Mississippi River to the Rocky Mountains from France in the **Louisiana Purchase.**

The British navy resumed seizing American merchant ships. They also seized American sailors for the royal navy, a practice known as **impressment.** Jefferson asked Congress to declare an **embargo,** suspending trade by ordering American ships to stay in port. The War of 1812 between Britain and the United States led to the end of tension with Britain. The United States won the war in 1815.

After the War of 1812, the Northeast became more industrialized, making it the most populous region in the country. However, the agricultural economy of the southern states relied on enslaved labor. The invention of the **cotton gin,** a machine that made cotton cheaper and faster to produce, led to a surge in cotton production.

In 1823, President Monroe issued the **Monroe Doctrine.** It declared that European monarchies had no business meddling with American republics. In return, the United States promised to stay out of European affairs.

Review Questions

1. What was a major foreign policy issue that confronted the United States after the French Revolution in 1789?

_____

_____

2. Why did the United States go to war with Britain in 1812?

_____

_____

Name _____ Class _____ Date _____

Note Taking Study Guide
DEMOCRACY, NATIONALISM, AND SECTIONALISM

Focus Question: What changes did Andrew Jackson bring to American political life?

As you read, note the effects of Jackson's presidency.

Andrew Jackson's Presidency

[Four blank boxes arranged vertically for note-taking]

Name _____ Class _____ Date _____

READING CHECK

What is the spoils system?

_____

_____

_____

VOCABULARY STRATEGY

What does the word *compelled* mean in the underlined sentence? Look for context clues in the surrounding words, phrases, and sentences. Circle the word below that is a synonym for *compelled.*

• forced
• recognized

READING SKILL

Understand Effects How did the Indian Removal Act affect the Cherokees?

_____

_____

_____

In 1824, **Andrew Jackson** ran for President. Jackson celebrated majority rule and the dignity of ordinary Americans. He rose at a time when national politics was becoming increasingly democratic. The 1820s saw a political shift in which any white man who paid a tax could vote in most states. Historians call this trend **Jacksonian democracy.** Although Jackson won the popular vote, the House of Representatives decided the election for John Quincy Adams.

In the election of 1828, Jackson triumphed over Adams. Once in office, Jackson replaced hundreds of government workers with Democratic activists. Jackson's foes denounced the **spoils system,** the practice of giving political jobs to party loyalists.

As President, Jackson urged Congress to pass the **Indian Removal Act** of 1830. This law sought to negotiate the peaceful exchange of Indian lands in the South for new lands in Indian Territory. In 1835, a small group of Cherokees signed an agreement with the government under which all Cherokees would leave the South. Though the majority of Cherokees protested, the federal government compelled 16,000 Cherokees to walk from the Southeast to Oklahoma along what came to be called the **Trail of Tears.**

Southerners benefited from Indian removal, but they opposed the federal government's adoption of protective tariffs. Jackson's Vice President, **John C. Calhoun** of South Carolina, violently opposed an especially high tariff in 1828. Calhoun championed **nullification,** the concept that states could overturn any federal law they deemed unconstitutional. The South Carolina government voted to nullify the tariff law and threatened to secede from the Union. Congress voted to give Jackson authority to use troops to enforce federal law in South Carolina. At the same time, Congress reduced the tariff and the crisis passed.

In 1832, Congress voted to renew the charter for the second Bank of the United States. Seeing the Bank as undemocratic and favoring a small number of rich investors, Jackson vetoed the renewal. Supporters of the Bank formed the Whig Party in 1832.

In 1836, voters elected Martin Van Buren to succeed Jackson. Soon after Van Buren took office, the economy suffered the **Panic of 1837,** the nation's worst economic depression to that time.

Review Questions

1. What was Jacksonian democracy?

_____

_____

2. How did Congress respond to South Carolina's vote to nullify the tariff law?

_____

_____

CHAPTER 2 — SECTION 2

Note Taking Study Guide
RELIGION AND REFORM

Focus Question: How did the Second Great Awakening affect life in the United States?

A. *As you read, note the main ideas relating to religion in the early 1800s.*

Religion in the Early 1800s		
Second Great Awakening	**Discrimination**	**Other Religious Movements**
• Camp meetings • • •	• • •	• • •

CHAPTER 2 SECTION 2

Note Taking Study Guide
RELIGION AND REFORM

Focus Question: How did the Second Great Awakening affect life in the United States?

B. *As you read, note the problems faced by reformers and what they accomplished.*

Causes	Efforts to Reform	Results
Educating all Americans		

CHAPTER **2** SECTION 2	**Section Summary** RELIGION AND REFORM

In the early 1800s, a powerful religious movement known as the **Second Great Awakening** swept America. One of the most influential revivalists was **Charles Grandison Finney.** The Second Great Awakening profoundly influenced American life. Religious fervor spurred many Americans to work for a variety of social reforms.

Heightened religious awareness also led to the formation of new religious groups. In New York, **Joseph Smith** organized the Church of Jesus Christ of Latter-day Saints in 1830. Smith's followers, known as Mormons, faced frequent discrimination. <u>After an angry mob murdered Smith, his successor, Brigham Young, led the Mormons to present-day Utah.</u>

Members of the Roman Catholic Church also faced harsh discrimination in the early 1800s. Many Protestants believed that Catholics would choose loyalty to the Pope over loyalty to the United States. In Philadelphia, anti-Catholic feelings led to a violent riot.

Jewish people were discriminated against as well. In the 1840s, a large number of Jewish immigrants came to America to escape political unrest in Europe. Yet, many state constitutions barred Jews from holding office.

One reformer who turned her religious ideals into action was **Dorothea Dix.** After discovering that patients suffering from mental illnesses were housed along with hardened criminals, Dix campaigned for humane hospitals for people with mental illnesses. Her work led directly to the creation of the first modern mental hospitals.

Religious motivation also played a key role in the **temperance movement,** the campaign to curb alcohol use. Temperance workers blamed many of the problems plaguing industrial America on the widespread use of alcohol.

Other reformers sought to improve education by working to establish free, tax-supported **public schools.** The most influential leader of the public school movement was **Horace Mann.** He argued for state oversight of local schools, standardized school calendars, and adequate school funding. He also worked to establish training to create a body of well-educated teachers.

Review Questions

1. Why did Catholics face harsh discrimination in the early 1800s?

_____

_____

2. What changes did Horace Mann work for?

_____

_____

READING CHECK

Who was Joseph Smith?

_____

_____

_____

VOCABULARY STRATEGY

What does the word *successor* mean in the underlined sentence? Look for context clues in the surrounding words, phrases, and sentences.

_____

_____

_____

READING SKILL

Understand Effects Describe one effect of the Second Great Awakening.

_____

_____

_____

CHAPTER 2 SECTION 3

Note Taking Study Guide
THE ANTISLAVERY MOVEMENT

Focus Question: What methods did Americans use to oppose slavery?

A. *As you read, summarize the ways people fought slavery.*

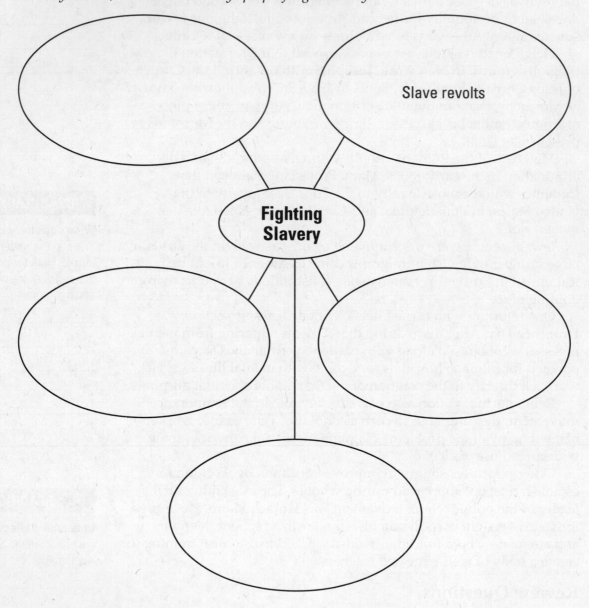

Slave revolts

Fighting Slavery

CHAPTER 2
SECTION 3

Note Taking Study Guide
THE ANTISLAVERY MOVEMENT

Focus Question: What methods did Americans use to oppose slavery?

B. *Use the chart below to contrast the different opinions held by abolitionists and people who opposed abolition.*

Debate Over Slavery	
Against	**For**
• Abolitionists believed that slavery was immoral. • •	• Slaveholders argued that slavery formed the basis of the South's economy. • • • •

Name _____ Class _____ Date _____

Section Summary
THE ANTISLAVERY MOVEMENT

Who led one of the most famous slave revolts?

_____

_____

_____

VOCABULARY STRATEGY

What does the word *inevitable* mean in the underlined sentence? Look for context clues in the surrounding words, phrases, and sentences. Circle the word below that is a synonym for *inevitable*.

• certain
• avoidable

READING SKILL

Summarize What were William Lloyd Garrison's views toward slavery?

_____

_____

_____

In the mid-1800s, some reformers tried to help the enslaved African Americans of the South. The most basic necessities of life were barely adequate for most enslaved African Americans. Most spent their lives laboring at backbreaking tasks. While the miserable conditions took an inevitable toll, most enslaved people maintained their hope and dignity through family traditions and religion.

Many enslaved people fought back against their oppressors. Resistance often took the form of sabotage, such as breaking tools or outwitting overseers. Sometimes, resistance became violent. The best-known slave revolt took place under the leadership of **Nat Turner.** Turner and his followers killed nearly 60 people before they were captured and executed.

Northern opponents of slavery, both black and white, risked their lives to help slaves escape to freedom through a loosely organized network known as the **underground railroad.** One of the most courageous conductors was **Harriet Tubman,** who made almost two dozen trips into the South, guiding hundreds of slaves to safety.

By the early 1800s, a growing number of **abolitionists** began to speak out. **William Lloyd Garrison** published an antislavery newspaper, *The Liberator.* Garrison advocated immediate emancipation and the extension of full political and social rights to African Americans. Although **Frederick Douglass** was born into slavery, he escaped to the North and became a powerful speaker at abolitionist meetings.

Women played key roles in most antislavery societies. **Angelina and Sarah Grimké,** daughters of a southern slaveholder, moved north to join the abolitionist movement.

In Massachusetts, writer and philosopher **Henry David Thoreau** spent a night in jail when he refused to pay a tax he felt supported slavery. Later, he wrote "Civil Disobedience," suggesting that people had the right to disobey laws they felt were unjust. The idea of **civil disobedience** would influence future leaders.

Despite the growing call of abolitionists, most Americans continued to oppose abolishing slavery. Defenders of slavery argued that slavery was necessary because it formed the foundation of the South's economy. The issue of slavery would soon prove to be a major factor in the division of the country.

Review Questions

1. What was the underground railroad?

_____

_____

2. Why did many Americans oppose the abolition of slavery?

_____

_____

Name _____ Class _____ Date _____

Focus Question: What steps did American women take to advance their rights in the mid-1800s?

As you read, record the causes and effects of the birth of the women's rights movement.

Effects

-
-

↑

Events

- Birth of women's rights movement
-
-

↑

Causes

- Limited rights
-
-

CHAPTER 2 SECTION 4

Section Summary
THE WOMEN'S MOVEMENT

READING CHECK

Which two women helped organize the Seneca Falls Convention?

_____

_____

_____

In the early 1800s, American women lacked many basic legal and economic rights. However, the drive to reform American society created by the Second Great Awakening provided new opportunities for women. Many joined reform groups sponsored by their churches. Women played leading roles in the great reform movements of the day, such as the temperance movement and the abolition movement. One of the most effective abolitionist lecturers was **Sojourner Truth,** a former slave who entranced audiences with her powerful speeches and arguments.

In the 1820s and 1830s, the Northeast was industrializing. This provided the first real economic opportunity for women outside the home. Thousands of young women went to work in the new mills and factories. By 1830, a few women's labor unions had formed.

In the 1830s, many urban middle-class northern women were freed from the burdens of housekeeping, giving them more time to think about the society in which they wanted to raise their children. Also, as more women became involved in the abolitionist movement, they began to see their own social restrictions as being comparable to slavery. They began to call for increased rights of their own.

VOCABULARY STRATEGY

What does the word *procuring* mean in the underlined sentence? Circle any words or phrases in the paragraph that help you figure out what *procuring* means.

_____

_____

_____

Women's rights reformers began to publish their ideas in pamphlets and books. In 1848, **Lucretia Mott** and **Elizabeth Cady Stanton** helped organize the nation's first Women's Rights Convention, held in Seneca Falls, New York. Often called the **Seneca Falls Convention,** the meeting attracted hundreds of men and women. The delegates adopted a **Declaration of Sentiments,** which called for greater educational opportunities for women, as well as for the right of women to control their own wages and property.

The Seneca Falls Convention marked the beginning of the **women's rights movement,** the campaign for equal rights for women, in the United States. It also inspired women such as **Susan B. Anthony,** whose involvement in the temperance and abolition movements motivated her to work for greater rights for women as well. <u>Anthony focused most of her efforts on procuring **suffrage,** or the right to vote.</u> By the mid-1800s, American women had laid the foundation for a future in which equality seemed a real possibility.

READING SKILL

Identify Causes and Effects
What were the effects of the Seneca Falls Convention?

_____

_____

_____

Review Questions

1. How did industrialization affect women's rights?

_____

_____

2. Explain how the abolitionist movement impacted the women's rights movement.

_____

_____

_____

CHAPTER 2 SECTION 5

Note Taking Study Guide

MANIFEST DESTINY

Focus Question: What were the causes and effects of territorial expansion?

As you read, record the main ideas relating to westward expansion.

I. **Looking Westward**

   A. Americans Seek New Land

      1. Southwest belongs to Mexico.

      2. _____

   B. _____

II. _____

   A. _____

   B. _____

III. _____

   A. _____

      1. _____

      2. _____

   B. _____

      1. _____

      2. _____

   C. _____

IV. _____

   A. _____

      1. _____

      2. _____

   B. _____

V. _____

   A. _____

      1. _____

      2. _____

   B. _____

   C. _____

      1. _____

      2. _____

CHAPTER 2 SECTION 5

Section Summary

MANIFEST DESTINY

READING CHECK

What discovery in 1848 led to a mass migration to California?

_____

_____

_____

VOCABULARY STRATEGY

What does the word *commencing* mean in the underlined sentence? Look for context clues in the surrounding words, phrases, and sentences. Circle the word below that is a synonym for *commencing*.

• remaining
• beginning

READING SKILL

Identify Main Ideas How did the idea of Manifest Destiny influence expansionists?

_____

_____

_____

By 1830, the United States had grown to include the Louisiana Purchase and Florida. Americans who favored territorial growth, known as **expansionists,** began to covet the Mexican provinces of New Mexico, Texas, and California. In an 1845 editorial, journalist John L. O'Sullivan expressed the idea that the United States was destined to own most or all of North America. The phrase **Manifest Destiny** became a rallying cry for expansionists.

American merchants and traders had already begun moving westward, blazing the Santa Fe Trail, the California Trail, and the **Oregon Trail.** Commencing in the spring, the journey covered nearly 2,000 miles over five months. Between 1840 and 1860, about 260,000 Americans crossed the continent to settle on the West Coast.

Americans had also begun to settle in Texas in the 1820s. In return for cheap land grants, settlers had to agree to become Mexican citizens. When Antonio López de Santa Anna seized power in Mexico in 1834, Texans, who wanted more control over their own affairs, rebelled. A year later, Texas declared its independence. For the next decade, a border war persisted between Texas and Mexico.

In December 1845, Congress narrowly voted to annex Texas as a slave state. President **James K. Polk** endorsed the Texan claim to the land south and west of the Nueces River. The Mexicans refused to recognize the annexation. When a Mexican patrol clashed with U.S. soldiers, killing eleven, Congress declared war on Mexico.

In this one-sided war, the United States won every major battle. In February 1848, the defeated Mexicans made peace in the **Treaty of Guadalupe Hidalgo.** The victors kept New Mexico and California, as well as secured the Rio Grande as the southern boundary of Texas. In 1853, the United States obtained another 29,640 square miles from Mexico in the **Gadsden Purchase.**

In 1848, workers found flecks of gold in the American River east of Sacramento. The news quickly spread to the East. By 1849, about 80,000 Americans were headed for California in a mass migration known as the **California Gold Rush.** The new Californians wanted to enter the Union quickly. When California applied for statehood, it renewed a heated debate over slavery between the North and South.

Review Questions

1. What did the United States gain in the Treaty of Guadalupe Hidalgo?

_____

_____

2. Why did Texans rebel when Santa Anna seized power in Mexico?

_____

_____

CHAPTER 3 SECTION 1

Note Taking Study Guide

THE UNION IN CRISIS

Focus Question: How did the issue of slavery divide the Union?

As you read, trace the sequence of events that led to the division of the Union.

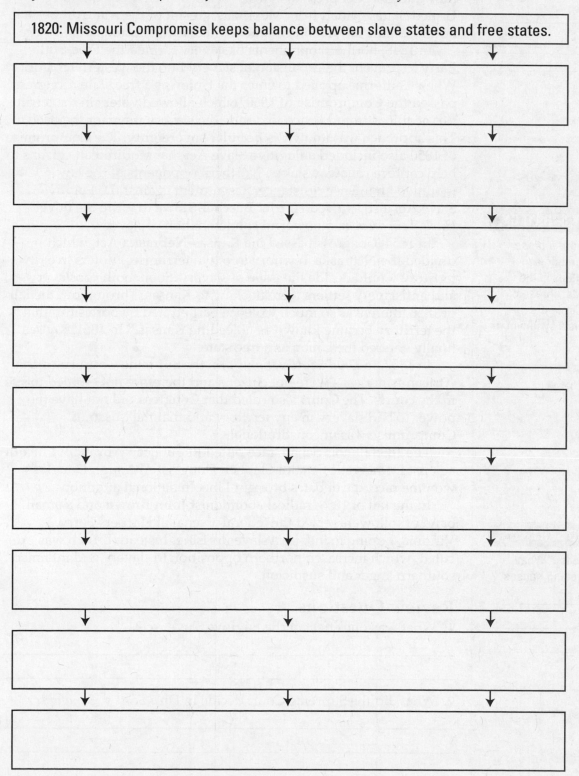

1820: Missouri Compromise keeps balance between slave states and free states.

Name _____ Class _____ Date _____

READING CHECK

What was popular sovereignty?

_____

_____

_____

During the Mexican-American War, the question of slavery in the West emerged as a major issue. In 1846, the **Wilmot Proviso** was introduced in Congress to ban slavery in any territory that the United States gained from Mexico as a result of the war. Although it never became law, it contributed to increasing tension over slavery.

In 1848, northern opponents of slavery formed the **Free-Soil Party** to prevent the expansion of slavery into the western territories. When California applied to enter the Union as a free state, Congress passed the **Compromise of 1850,** which allowed voters in the territories acquired from Mexico to decide the slavery issue for themselves. This approach was known as **popular sovereignty.** The Compromise of 1850 also included a Fugitive Slave Act that required all citizens to help capture runaway slaves. Northern opponents of the law mounted an intense resistance. Resentment against the Fugitive Slave Act also spurred **Harriet Beecher Stowe** to write the novel *Uncle Tom's Cabin,* a powerful condemnation of slavery.

In 1854, Congress passed the **Kansas-Nebraska Act,** which divided the Nebraska Territory into two territories. Voters in each territory would decide the issue of slavery. Soon, both proslavery and antislavery settlers were flocking to Kansas. Throughout the fall of 1856, there was so much violence perpetrated by both sides that the territory became known as "Bleeding Kansas." In 1861, Kansas finally entered the Union as a free state.

In 1857, in *Dred Scott* **v.** *Sandford,* the Supreme Court ruled that African Americans were not citizens and therefore not entitled to sue in the courts. The Court also ruled that Congress did not have the power to ban slavery in any territory and that the Missouri Compromise was unconstitutional.

The 1858 Illinois Senate race pitted Republican **Abraham Lincoln** against Democratic Senator Stephen Douglas. Although Douglas won the race, the debates brought Lincoln national attention.

In the fall of 1859, radical abolitionist **John Brown** and a small band of followers seized the federal arsenal at Harpers Ferry, Virginia, hoping to inspire a slave uprising. Instead, Brown was executed, which increased northern opposition to slavery and inflamed southern anger and suspicion.

VOCABULARY STRATEGY

What does the word *intense* mean in the underlined sentence? Look for clues in the surrounding words, phrases, and sentences. Circle the word below that is a synonym for *intense.*

- weak
- extreme

READING SKILL

Recognize Sequence What event led to "Bleeding Kansas"?

_____

_____

_____

Review Questions

1. What was one effect of the Fugitive Slave Act?

_____

_____

2. What did the Supreme Court decide in *Dred Scott* v. *Sandford?*

_____

_____

Focus Question: How did the Union finally collapse into a civil war?

Fill in the cause-and-effect chart below to show the events that led to secession.

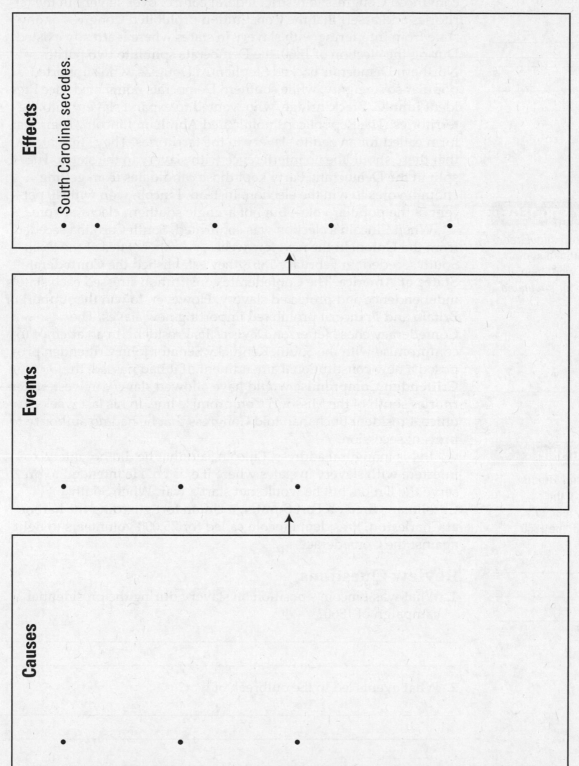

Effects

- South Carolina secedes.
-
-
-
-

Events

-
-
-

Causes

-
-
-

CHAPTER 3 SECTION 2

Section Summary
LINCOLN, SECESSION, AND WAR

In 1860, anxiety ran high in both the North and the South as the presidential election approached. Mississippi Senator **Jefferson Davis** convinced Congress to restrict federal control over slavery in the territories and assert that the Constitution prohibited Congress or any state from interfering with slavery in states where it already existed. During the election of 1860, the Democrats split into two parties. Northern Democrats backed Stephen A. Douglas, who supported popular sovereignty, while southern Democrats nominated Vice President **John C. Breckinridge,** who wanted to expand slavery into the territories. The Republicans nominated Abraham Lincoln. Their platform called for an end to slavery in the territories. They stipulated that there should be no interference with slavery in the states. The split in the Democratic Party kept those candidates from getting enough votes to win the election. Instead, Lincoln won with 40 percent of the popular vote—but not a single southern electoral vote.

When Lincoln's election was confirmed, South Carolina seceded from the Union. In the next few weeks, six other states of the Deep South seceded. In February 1861, they established the **Confederate States of America.** The Confederate constitution stressed each state's independence and protected slavery. However, to win the support of Britain and France, it prohibited importing new slaves. The Confederacy chose Jefferson Davis as its President. In an attempt to compromise with the South, Kentucky Senator John Crittenden proposed a new constitutional amendment. If it had passed, the **Crittenden Compromise** would have allowed slavery in western territories south of the Missouri Compromise line. In his last weeks in office, President Buchanan told Congress that he had no authority to prevent secession.

In his inaugural address, Lincoln said that he did not intend to interfere with slavery in states where it existed. He intended to preserve the Union, but he would not start a war. When South Carolinians fired on **Fort Sumter,** a Union fort guarding the harbor at Charleston, President Lincoln called for 75,000 volunteers to fight against the Confederacy.

Review Questions

1. What was Lincoln's position on slavery during the presidential campaign of 1860?

_____

_____

2. What events led to the outbreak of war?

_____

_____

Name _____ Class _____ Date _____

Focus Question: What factors and events led to the Union victory in the Civil War?

A. *As you read, identify the events and developments that led to the final Union victory in the Civil War.*

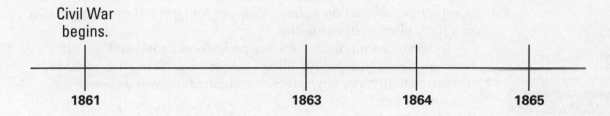

Civil War begins.

1861　　　　　　　　**1863**　　**1864**　　　　**1865**

B. *As you read, note effects of the war on the North and South.*

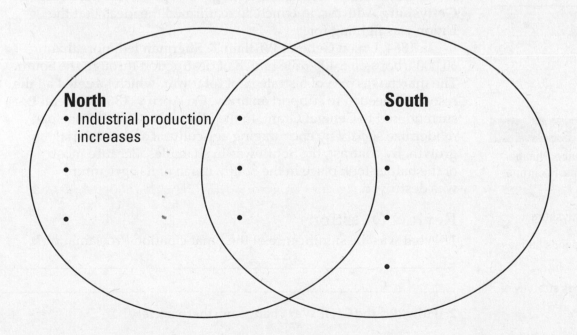

North
- Industrial production increases
-
-

South
-
-
-
-

CHAPTER 3 SECTION 3

Section Summary
THE CIVIL WAR

Name the speech that President Lincoln gave that reaffirmed the ideas the Union was fighting for.

_____

_____

_____

What does the word *anticipated* mean in the underlined sentence? The word *guessed* is a synonym of *anticipated.* Use this synonym to help you figure out the meaning of *anticipated.*

_____

_____

_____

Recognize Sequence Number the following events in chronological order.

_____ Battle of Gettysburg

_____ Lincoln suspends habeas corpus.

_____ Sherman uses strategy of total war.

Between 1861 and 1865, the Union and the Confederacy fought each other in the Civil War. The urbanized North was able to produce the supplies necessary to wage war. Given such advantages, northerners anticipated a quick victory. By contrast, the more rural South had skillful and experienced military leaders, such as General **Robert E. Lee.**

The North adopted a strategy known as the **Anaconda Plan,** which aimed to starve the South into submission. For its part, the South hoped to wait out the war until northerners became tired of fighting. Although each side won some battles, a stalemate developed. The combination of new weapons and limited medical care led to a high number of casualties.

In 1863, Lincoln issued the **Emancipation Proclamation,** which freed all slaves in areas rebelling against the Union. Although it did not actually free any slaves, it redefined the war as being "about slavery."

Some northerners opposed Lincoln's conduct of the war. To deal with dissent, Lincoln suspended the constitutional right of **habeas corpus,** which guarantees that no one can be held in prison without specific charges being filed. Meanwhile, the South was struggling with economic problems. Doubts about the true value of Confederate money led to severe **inflation,** or price increases.

In the summer of 1863, Union General **Ulysses S. Grant** won several victories and split apart Confederate territory. In the East, Confederate troops were defeated in the **Battle of Gettysburg.** A few months later, President Lincoln gave a speech known as the **Gettysburg Address,** in which he reaffirmed the ideas that the Union was fighting for.

In 1864, Union General **William T. Sherman** led more than 60,000 troops on a 400-mile march of destruction through the South. The march was part of a strategy of **total war,** which targeted all the resources needed to support an army. On April 9, 1865, General Lee surrendered to General Grant. In the North, the Civil War helped modernize society by encouraging agricultural and industrial growth. By contrast, the South was in shambles. Because most of the battles took place in the South, much of its agriculture was destroyed.

Review Questions

1. What was the significance of the Emancipation Proclamation?

_____

_____

2. How did the Civil War change northern society?

_____

_____

Name _____ Class _____ Date _____

Focus Question: What were the immediate and long-term effects of Reconstruction?

As you read, identify the political, social, and economic aspects of Reconstruction.

Political	Social	Economic
• Radical Republicans clash with President. • • • •	• • • • • •	• Sharecropping develops. •

Name _____ Class _____ Date _____

Which amendment ended slavery?

_____

_____

_____

What is the meaning of the word *status* in the underlined sentence? Circle any words or phrases in the surrounding sentences that help you figure out the meaning of the word.

_____

_____

_____

Categorize Which aspects of Reconstruction were unsuccessful?

_____

_____

_____

During the Civil War, Union politicians debated ways to achieve **Reconstruction,** or bringing the South back into the Union. For President Lincoln, the major goal was to reunify the nation. Some congressional leaders favored a harsh Reconstruction plan. However, Lincoln and Congress agreed to create the **Freedmen's Bureau,** an agency designed to aid freed slaves and relieve the South's needs.

On April 14, 1865, Lincoln was assassinated and Vice President **Andrew Johnson** assumed the presidency. Johnson wanted to restore southern political power, if southerners accepted the **Thirteenth Amendment,** which ended slavery. In contrast, **Radical Republicans** wanted to punish the South and protect full rights for African Americans. Johnson and the Radicals in Congress clashed repeatedly. In 1868, Congress began **impeachment** proceedings against Johnson. Although Johnson was not removed from office, Ulysses S. Grant was elected President a few months later.

With Congress firmly in their control, Radical Republicans divided the South into five military districts. As a condition of readmission to the Union, states had to grant the vote to African American men. Radicals also passed the **Fourteenth Amendment,** which guaranteed full citizenship status and rights to every person born in the United States. In 1870, the **Fifteenth Amendment** was passed, guaranteeing male citizens the right to vote.

Most black farmers came to work under a system called **sharecropping.** In return for advancing materials to the sharecroppers, landowners received a share of the crop's value. Often, the crops did not cover the cost, leaving most sharecroppers in debt. Meanwhile, organized secret societies, such as the **Ku Klux Klan,** used terror and violence to prevent African Americans from voting.

The presidential election of 1876 signaled the end of Reconstruction. In exchange for becoming President, Republican Rutherford B. Hayes promised to withdraw all remaining federal troops from the South. Although the nation was reunited and the South began to rebuild, the political rights of African Americans continued to erode. **Segregation,** or legal separation of the races, became the law in all southern states.

Review Questions

1. What did Rutherford B. Hayes promise in return for becoming President?

_____

_____

2. How did President Johnson's approach to Reconstruction differ from that of Radical Republicans?

_____

_____

Name _____ Class _____ Date _____

Note Taking Study Guide

CHAPTER **4** SECTION 1

TECHNOLOGY AND INDUSTRIAL GROWTH

Focus Question: How did industrialization and new technology affect the economy and society?

As you read, record the causes and effects of industrialization in the chart below.

Causes		Effects
•		•
•		•
•		•
•		•
•		•
•	**Event**	•
•	Industrialization	•
•		•
•		•
		•
		•

CHAPTER 4 SECTION 1

Section Summary

TECHNOLOGY AND INDUSTRIAL GROWTH

The Civil War encouraged industrial growth by challenging industries to make products more quickly and efficiently than they had been made before. The country's growth was also fueled by its vast supply of natural resources. In addition, industries had a huge workforce to fuel growth. After the Civil War, large numbers of Europeans, and some Asians, immigrated to the United States.

Entrepreneurs fueled industrialization. Capitalism is a system in which individuals own most businesses. The heroes of this system were **entrepreneurs,** or people who invest money in a product or enterprise in order to make a profit.

Government encouraged the success of businesses in the late 1800s. To encourage the buying of American goods, Congress enacted **protective tariffs,** or taxes that would make imported goods cost more than those made locally. The government also encouraged **laissez faire** policies, which allowed business to operate under minimal government regulation.

Thomas Edison received more than 1,000 **patents** for new inventions. Edison and his team invented the light bulb. George Westinghouse developed technology to send electricity over long distances. Electricity lit streets and powered homes and factories. Alexander Graham Bell patented the telephone. By 1900, there were more than one million telephones in the United States.

The **Bessemer process** created strong but lightweight steel that made possible innovations, including skyscrapers and **suspension bridges.** As railroads expanded, they stimulated new technology. To help trains set schedules, the globe was divided into twenty-four **time zones.** Electric streetcars, commuter trains, and subways appeared in major cities. As a result, American suburbs grew.

To meet the growing demand for goods, factory owners developed systems known as **mass production** for turning out large numbers of products quickly and inexpensively.

Industrialization touched every aspect of American life. Farms became mechanized. Mass production meant people had easy access to goods. As the United States grew as an economic power, it became more involved in the affairs of other nations.

Review Questions

1. How did entrepreneurs encourage industrialization?

_____

_____

2. What innovations were made possible by the Bessemer process?

_____

_____

Name _____ Class _____ Date _____

Focus Question: How did big business shape the American economy in the late 1800s and early 1900s?

A. *Record supporting details about the rise of American big business in the chart below.*

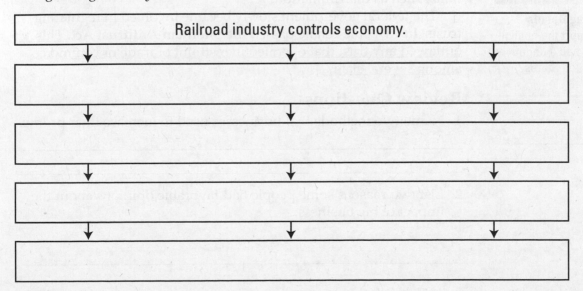

Rise of Big Business

Corporations

-
-
-
-
-

Debates

-
-
-
-
-

B. *As you read, record details about how the government gradually became involved in regulating industry.*

Railroad industry controls economy.

↓   ↓   ↓

[ ]

↓   ↓   ↓

[ ]

↓   ↓   ↓

[ ]

↓   ↓   ↓

[ ]

CHAPTER 4 · SECTION 2

Section Summary
THE RISE OF BIG BUSINESS

Name one social condition that people used Social Darwinism to justify.

_____

_____

_____

What does the word *restraint* mean in the underlined sentence? The terms *control* and *command* are synonyms of *restraint.* Use these synonyms to help you figure out the meaning of *restraint.*

_____

_____

_____

Identify Supporting Details
What details support the opinion that big business had a negative impact on the United States?

_____

_____

_____

To take advantage of larger markets, investors developed a form of group ownership known as a **corporation.** In a corporation, a number of people share ownership of a business. Corporations had access to huge amounts of money, allowing them to fund new technology or enter new industries.

Corporations worked to maximize profits in several ways. Some corporations tried to gain a **monopoly,** or complete control of a product or service. Other corporations worked to eliminate competition by forming **cartels.** In this arrangement, businesses making the same product agreed to limit their production and thus keep prices high. Another way to increase profits was to create a giant company with lower production costs. This system of consolidating many firms in the same business is called **horizontal integration. John D. Rockefeller, Andrew Carnegie,** and other businessmen also increased their power by gaining control of the many different businesses that make up all phases of a product's development. This process, called **vertical integration,** allowed businessmen to reduce costs and charge higher costs to competitors.

Gradually, consumers, workers, and the federal government came to feel that systems like **trusts,** cartels, and monopolies gave powerful businessmen an unfair advantage. At the same time, many people believed that business leaders served the nation positively. Factories, steel mills, and railroads provided jobs. The development of efficient business practices and industrialists' support for developing technology benefited the nation's economy, shaping the United States into a strong international leader. Finally, many business leaders were important philanthropists.

Charles Darwin's theory of survival of the fittest was applied to the world of American capitalism and was called **Social Darwinism.** People used Social Darwinism to justify all sorts of beliefs and conditions, such as discrimination.

The federal government slowly became involved in regulating trusts. In 1890, the Senate passed the **Sherman Antitrust Act.** <u>This act outlawed any trust that operated in restraint of trade or commerce among several states.</u>

Review Questions

1. Name two methods that businesses used to increase their profits.

_____

_____

2. List two reasons some people had favorable opinions about the impact of big business.

_____

_____

Name _____ Class _____ Date _____

Focus Question: How did the rise of labor unions shape relations among workers, big business, and government?

Record the main ideas about the rise of organized labor in the concept web below.

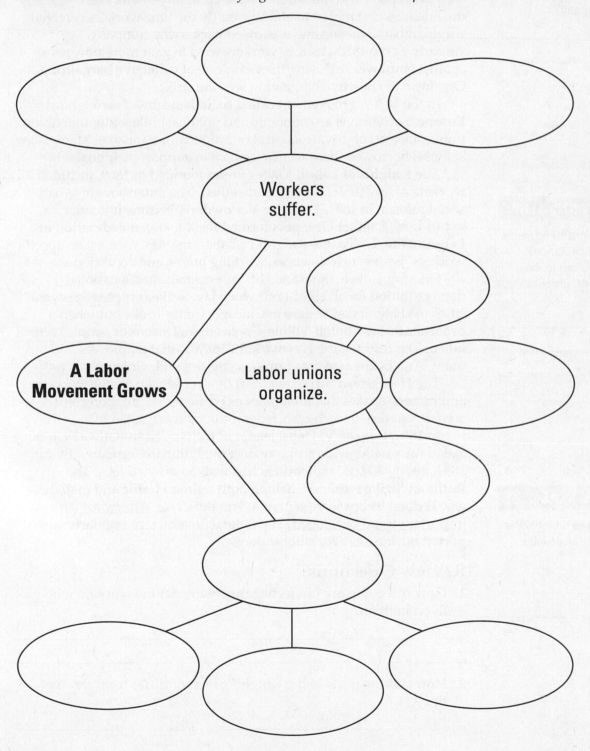

CHAPTER 4 SECTION 3

Section Summary
THE ORGANIZED LABOR MOVEMENT

READING CHECK

Who was the leader that called for a nationwide strike against the Pullman Company?

_____

_____

_____

VOCABULARY STRATEGY

What does the word *trend* mean in the underlined sentence? Look for context clues in the surrounding words, phrases, and sentences.

_____

_____

_____

READING SKILL

Identify Main Ideas Identify the main goals of organized labor.

_____

_____

_____

Industrial growth produced wealth for business owners. However, factory workers toiled long hours in dirty workhouses known as **sweatshops.** Many miners were forced to live in communities near their workplace. The housing in these **company towns** was owned by the business and rented to employees. By the time workers received wages, most of the income was owed back to the company. As early as the 1820s, factory workers tried to gain more power against employers by using the technique of **collective bargaining.** One form of collective bargaining was the strike.

In the 1830s, a movement called **socialism** spread throughout Europe. Socialism is an economic and political philosophy that favors public, instead of private, control of property and income. Many labor activists borrowed ideas from socialism to support their goals.

The **Knights of Labor,** a labor union founded in 1869, included all workers of any trade, skilled or unskilled. The union sought broad social reform. In 1881, **Terrence V. Powderly** became its leader.

In 1886, **Samuel Gompers** formed the **American Federation of Labor (AFL).** Unlike the Knights of Labor, the AFL focused on specific workers' issues such as wages, working hours, and conditions.

On May 1, 1886, thousands of workers mounted a national demonstration for an eight-hour workday. Strikes erupted in several cities. At Haymarket Square in Chicago, frenzy broke out when a protester threw a bomb, killing a policeman. Dozens of people were killed. The result of the **Haymarket Riot** was that employers and many Americans associated union activities with violence.

The **Homestead Strike** was part of an epidemic of steelworkers' and miners' strikes that took place as economic depression crept across America. In each case, federal troops were called in.

In 1893, **Eugene V. Debs,** leader of the American Railway Union, called for a nationwide strike against the Pullman Company. By June 1894, nearly 300,000 railworkers had walked off their jobs. The **Pullman Strike** escalated, halting both railroad traffic and mail delivery. Federal troops were sent in to end the strike. <u>Afterward, an important trend developed.</u> The federal government regularly supported businesses over labor unions.

Review Questions

1. How did company towns negatively impact the workers who lived in them?

_____

_____

2. How did the goals of the Knights of Labor differ from those of the AFL?

_____

_____

CHAPTER 5
SECTION 1

Note Taking Study Guide
THE NEW IMMIGRANTS

Focus Question: Why did immigrants come to the United States, and what impact did they have upon society?

Record the main ideas of the section in the outline below.

I. **New Immigrants Come to America**
   A. _____
   B. _____
   C. _____

II. **Immigrants Decide to Leave Home**
   A. _____
      1. _____
      2. _____
   B. _____
      1. _____
      2. _____

III. _____
   A. _____
   B. _____
      1. _____
      2. _____

IV. _____
   A. _____
   B. _____
      1. _____
      2. _____
   C. _____
      1. _____
      2. _____

Name _____ Class _____ Date _____

How did most immigrants travel to America?

_____

_____

_____

What does the word *preliminary* mean in the underlined sentence? Use context clues in the surrounding words and phrases to help you figure out the meaning of *preliminary*.

_____

_____

_____

Identify Main Ideas Discuss the challenges immigrants faced in America.

_____

_____

_____

Many early American immigrants were Protestants from northern and western Europe or German and Irish Catholics. Many were skilled and educated, and came as families to work on farms. In the 1870s, **"new" immigrants** from southern and eastern Europe came to America. They often came alone, were unskilled and poor, Catholic or Jewish, and settled in cities rather than on farms.

Two types of factors lead to immigration. Push factors compel people to leave their homes. These include famine, war, and persecution. Pull factors, such as economic opportunities or religious freedom, draw people to a new place. Land reform and low prices for grain pushed farmers in Mexico, Poland, China, and Italy to leave. Wars in China and eastern Europe, and religious persecution in eastern Europe were also push factors. Inexpensive land and employment opportunities were examples of pull factors.

Most immigrants traveled in **steerage,** the crowded and dirty lower decks of steamships. There, illness spread quickly. Shipowners did a preliminary medical screening before passengers boarded. Still, immigration officials met ships at American ports to determine who could stay. Immigrants had to be healthy and prove that they had money, a skill, or a sponsor. Beginning in 1892, most European immigrants were processed at **Ellis Island** in New York Harbor. Chinese and other Asian immigrants were processed at **Angel Island,** which opened in 1910, in San Francisco Bay.

Volunteer organizations tried to help immigrants blend into the **"melting pot"** of American society. Still, many immigrants held on to their traditions. Newcomers often faced **nativism,** the belief that native-born white Americans were superior to newcomers. Immigrants competed for jobs and housing, and their religious and cultural differences made native-born Americans suspicious. Hostility toward Chinese laborers led Congress to pass the **Chinese Exclusion Act** in 1882, limiting the civil rights of Chinese immigrants and forbidding their naturalization. Despite opposition, immigrants fueled industrial growth, elected politicians, and made their traditions part of American culture.

Review Questions

1. Describe the pull factors that drew immigrants to America.

_____

_____

2. What characteristics set new immigrants apart from earlier immigrants?

_____

_____

Name _____ Class _____ Date _____

Note Taking Study Guide

CITIES EXPAND AND CHANGE

Focus Question: What challenges did city dwellers face, and how did they meet them?

Record the main ideas of this section in the following flowchart.

Cities Expand and Change

Urbanization	Technology	Problems
•	•	•
•	•	•
•	•	•
•	•	•
•	•	•
		•

CHAPTER **5** SECTION 2	## Section Summary
	CITIES EXPAND AND CHANGE

VOCABULARY STRATEGY

What does the word *innovations* mean in the underlined sentence? Look for context clues in the surrounding words and phrases. Circle any words or phrases in the paragraph that help you figure out what *innovations* means.

_____

_____

_____

READING SKILL

Identify Main Ideas Describe the problems caused by rapid growth and the steps that cities took to solve them.

_____

_____

_____

America went through **urbanization** in the late nineteenth century. The number of cities and of people living in them greatly increased. Major cities were clustered in the Northeast, on the Pacific Coast, and along Midwestern waterways. These centers of manufacturing and transportation were connected by new railroad lines.

In addition to immigrants looking for factory work, many **rural-to-urban migrants** moved to cities. Making a living by farming was increasingly difficult, and cities offered excitement and variety. Cities also offered greater job possibilities for women. Children had the opportunity to attend school.

To meet increased demands for water, sewers, schools, and safety in growing cities, Americans developed new technologies. These innovations included electric trolleys, subways, and **skyscrapers,** tall buildings that housed large numbers of offices. **Elisha Otis** developed a safety elevator that would not fall if the lifting rope broke. Streetcars powered by electricity revolutionized transportation, and **mass transit,** public transportation systems capable of carrying a large number of people inexpensively, reshaped the nation. Those who could afford it moved to cleaner and quieter streetcar **suburbs** on the outskirts of cities and rode mass transit into the city for work and entertainment.

Cities created different zones for heavy industry, financial institutions, and residences. They also built public places, such as libraries, government buildings, universities, and parks. Landscape engineer **Frederick Law Olmsted** was hired to design a number of parks including New York City's Central Park.

With the growth of cities came a number of problems. Cities were filthy and trash-filled. Most urban workers lived in overcrowded, low-cost multifamily housing called **tenements.** With few windows and little sanitation, they were unhealthy and dangerous places. Open fireplaces and gas lighting enabled fires to quickly rip through cities. Unlit streets also posed dangers to those coming from or going to work. In response, many cities created firefighting teams and police forces. City planners began regulating housing, sanitation, and sewers.

Review Questions

1. Describe the technologies that improved life in the city.

_____

_____

2. Why did people move to cities?

_____

_____

CHAPTER 5
SECTION 3

Note Taking Study Guide

SOCIAL AND CULTURAL TRENDS

Focus Question: What luxuries did cities offer to the middle class?

Record the main ideas of this section below.

Consumerism	Mass Culture	Entertainment
•	•	•
•	•	•
•	•	•
•	•	•
•		•
		•
		•
		•

CHAPTER 5 SECTION 3
Section Summary
SOCIAL AND CULTURAL TRENDS

In *The Gilded Age,* novelist **Mark Twain** depicted American society in the late 1800s as gilded, or having a rotten core covered with gold paint. Most Americans were not as cynical. More people worked for wages, and more products were available than ever before and at lower prices, leading to a culture of **conspicuous consumerism.**

Department stores opened in the late 1850s. They used advertising to sell high-quality goods at fair prices. The postal service lowered shipping rates and offered free rural delivery, leading to a mail-order boom. Companies began creating trademarks with distinctive logos and for the first time, consumers began buying brand-name goods.

Transportation, advertising, and communication helped create a **mass culture** in which Americans became more and more alike in their consumption patterns. Household gadgets, toys, and food preferences were often the same from house to house. Newspapers both reflected and helped create mass culture, including **Joseph Pulitzer**'s morning paper, the *World.* Pulitzer believed that newspapers should inform people and stir up controversy. **William Randolph Hearst** mimicked Pulitzer's sensationalist tactics in his newspaper, the *Morning Journal.* However, some novelists like **Horatio Alger** focused on moral issues. Ethnic and special-interest publications catered to urban dwellers, especially immigrants. Newspapers were successful, in part, because more people could read. Public education expanded rapidly, and by 1900, the literacy rate reached nearly 90 percent.

Urban areas became centers for new types of entertainment. Amusement parks were built close to cities around the country. Touring outdoor shows like "Buffalo Bill's Wild West Show" drew crowds. Religious-inspired entertainment, including the Chautauqua Circuit, also grew in popularity. **Vaudeville** shows, made up of musical drama, songs, and off-color comedy, were found throughout the country. Movie theaters introduced motion pictures, charging a nickel for admission. Baseball, horse racing, bicycle racing, boxing, and football became popular spectator sports.

Review Questions
1. Describe how a mass culture developed in America.

_____

_____

2. How did shopping change in America?

_____

_____

Name _____ Class _____ Date _____

Focus Question: How did the southern economy and society change after the Civil War?

As you read, fill in the concept web below with details about how the South changed after the Civil War.

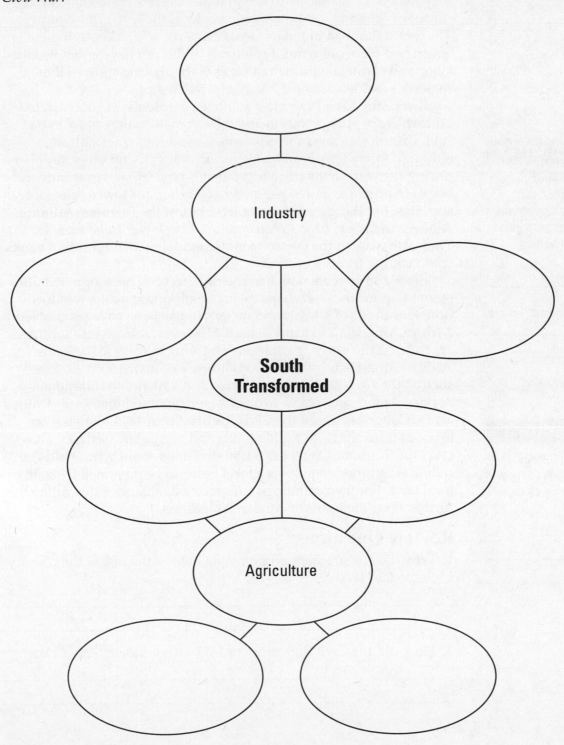

Name _____ Class _____ Date _____

What were the goals of the Farmers' Alliance?

_____

_____

_____

What does the word *component* mean in the underlined sentence? Use context clues in the surrounding sentences to help you figure out the meaning of *component*.

_____

_____

_____

Identify Supporting Details
Provide three examples of how the southern economy changed after the Civil War.

_____

_____

_____

Before the Civil War, the South had shipped its raw materials abroad or to the North for processing. In the 1880s, northern money helped the South to build its own factories. <u>Transportation was also a key component of industrialization.</u> As southern rail lines expanded, they joined rural areas with urban hubs. Despite these changes, the southern economy continued to lag behind the rest of the country. The South first had to repair the damages of war. Although the South had plenty of natural resources, it did not have enough skilled labor and capital investment. Wages were low and most of the region's wealth was in the hands of a few people.

Before the Civil War, most southern planters had concentrated on **cash crops** such as cotton and tobacco, which they grew to be sold. Cotton remained the centerpiece of southern agriculture, although many European textile factories had found other suppliers during the war, so the price had fallen. In the 1870s, Texas farmers began to organize and to negotiate as a group for lower prices for supplies. Local organizations joined to form the **Farmers' Alliance.** Alliance members tried to force railroads to lower freight prices. They also wanted the government to regulate the interest that banks could charge for loans.

Black southerners now had the right to vote. New opportunities opened up for them. Perhaps the most important goal was education. Hundreds of schools and dozens of teachers' colleges enabled African Americans to learn to read. However, some white southerners focused their own frustrations on trying to reverse the gains African Americans had achieved during Reconstruction. Groups such as the Ku Klux Klan used terror and violence to intimidate African Americans. Many African American freedoms were whittled away. Congress passed the **Civil Rights Act of 1875** to guarantee black patrons the right to ride trains and use public facilities. However, the Supreme Court ruled that decisions about who could use public accommodations was a local issue, to be governed by state or local laws. Southern municipalities took advantage of this ruling to further limit the rights of African Americans.

Review Questions

1. Why did the southern economy lag behind the rest of the country in the late 1800s?

_____

_____

2. How did the Civil Rights Act of 1875 affect African Americans?

_____

_____

Name _____ Class _____ Date _____

Focus Question: How did the pressures of westward expansion impact Native Americans?

A. *As you read, fill in the concept web below with details about Native Americans west of the Mississippi.*

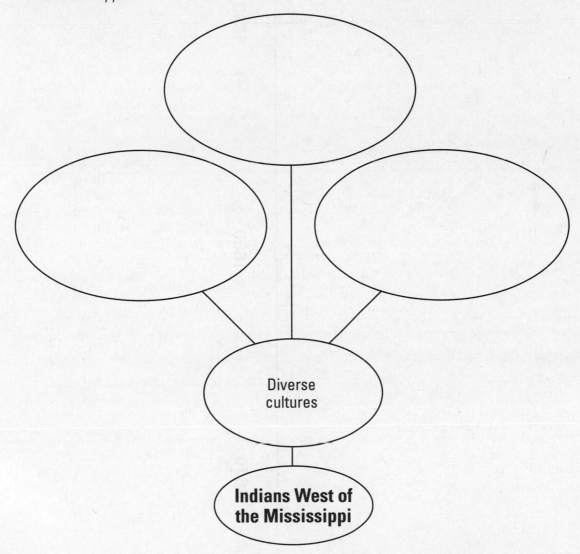

Diverse cultures

Indians West of the Mississippi

Name _____ Class _____ Date _____

Focus Question: How did the pressures of westward expansion impact Native Americans?

B. *Use the timeline below to record important dates and events in the Indian Wars.*

1890

1880

1870

1864
Sand Creek
Massacre

1860

CHAPTER 6 SECTION 2

Section Summary
WESTWARD EXPANSION AND THE AMERICAN INDIANS

By the end of the Civil War, about 250,000 Indians lived in the region west of the Mississippi River known as "The Great American Desert." Geography influenced their cultural diversity, but all Indian cultures saw themselves as part of nature and considered it sacred. By contrast, many whites viewed the land as a resource to produce wealth. In the early 1800s, the government began to move Native Americans out of the way of white settlers. Things changed when gold and silver were discovered in Indian Territory. In 1851, the government began to restrict Indians to smaller areas. By the late 1860s, they were forced to live on **reservations,** where they lacked adequate resources.

In 1864, Colorado militia attacked an unarmed camp of Cheyenne and Arapaho. The **Sand Creek Massacre,** as it came to be known, spawned more warfare between Plains Indians and white settlers. When gold was discovered in the Black Hills, the Sioux, led by chiefs Crazy Horse and **Sitting Bull,** tried to drive white prospectors out of Sioux lands. At the **Battle of Little Big Horn** in June 1876, the Sioux killed all the United States Army cavalry forces led by George Custer. In 1877, the Nez Percés tried to escape to Canada when the federal government wanted to relocate them to a smaller reservation. The Nez Percés were captured just short of the border and relocated to a barren reservation in Oklahoma. Their leader, **Chief Joseph,** traveled twice to Washington, D.C., to lobby for mercy for his people. In 1890, hostilities broke out at **Wounded Knee,** South Dakota, over a religious revival based on the Ghost Dance. The cavalry outgunned the Indians.

Policymakers hoped that Indians would become farmers and **assimilate** into national life by adopting the culture and civilization of whites. In 1887, Congress passed the **Dawes General Allotment Act.** It replaced the reservation system with a system under which each Indian family was granted a 160-acre farmstead. To help speed assimilation, missionaries and other reformers established boarding schools where Indian children were taught to live by the rules of white America.

Review Questions

1. What differing beliefs caused white settlers and Native Americans to clash over land use?

_____

_____

2. What measures were taken to assimilate Native Americans into national life?

_____

_____

READING CHECK

Who was Chief Joseph?

_____

_____

_____

VOCABULARY STRATEGY

What does the word *adequate* mean in the underlined sentence? Read the underlined sentence aloud, but leave out the word *adequate.* What word could you use in its place? Use this strategy to help you figure out the meaning of *adequate.*

_____

_____

_____

READING SKILL

Recognize Sequence How did life change for Native Americans after gold and silver were discovered in Indian Territory?

_____

_____

_____

Note Taking Study Guide

CHAPTER 6 SECTION 3

TRANSFORMING THE WEST

Focus Question: What economic and social factors changed the West after the Civil War?

Use the chart below to record details about changes in the West.

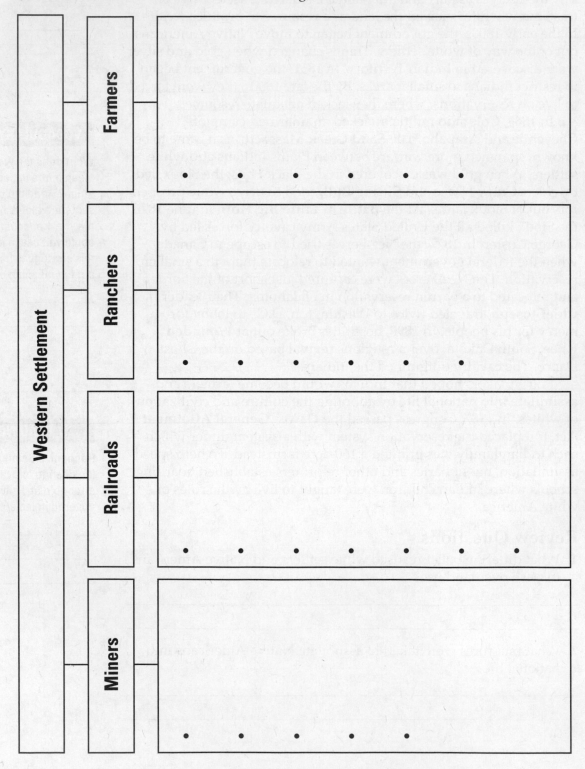

CHAPTER 6 SECTION 3

Section Summary

TRANSFORMING THE WEST

Mining was the first great boom in the West. Mining camps sprang up quickly. <u>To administer justice, miners set up rules of conduct and procedures for settling disputes.</u> At first, mining was done by individuals who found the minerals in the surface soil or a streambed. By the 1870s, big companies took over the industry. The federal government supported these companies by providing them with cheap land and patents for new inventions. Mining wealth helped fuel the nation's industrial development.

As industry in the West grew, the need for a **transcontinental railroad** linking the East and the West became apparent. Congress supported its construction in two ways: It provided money in the form of loans and made **land grants,** giving builders wide stretches of land, alternating on each side of the track route. Work on the railroad began in 1863 and was completed in 1869. Railroads had far-reaching effects. They tied the nation together, moved products and people across the continent, and spurred industrial development. They also stimulated the growth of towns and cities and intensified the demand for Indian land.

Cattle ranching was another western boom. With railroads to move meat to eastern markets, the race was on for land and water. At first, cattle were raised on the **open-range** system. Property was not fenced in, and cattle were branded to identify them. Cowboys learned much from the Mexican vaqueros. By the mid-1880s, the heyday of open-ranching came to an end.

The Great Plains was the last part of the country to be heavily settled by whites. Under the **Homestead Act,** passed in 1862, the government offered farm plots to homesteaders. Some new settlers were former slaves called **"Exodusters."** They followed an exodus out of bondage to a new "promised land" in Kansas and Oklahoma, where they planted crops and founded several all-black towns.

From the 1850s onward, the West had the widest diversity of people in the nation. Conflict came in many forms. There were ethnic tensions. Ranchers often belittled homesteaders. The last major land rush took place in 1889, when the federal government opened Oklahoma to homesteaders. The next year, the national census concluded that there was no longer a "frontier."

Review Questions

1. How did the railroads affect the settlement of the West?

_____

_____

2. How did ranching change over time?

_____

_____

READING CHECK

Who were the Exodusters?

_____

_____

_____

VOCABULARY STRATEGY

What does the word *administer* mean in the underlined sentence? Look for context clues in the surrounding words, phrases, and sentences. Circle the word below that is a synonym for *administer*.

- manage
- dispute

READING SKILL

Identify Main Ideas Why were early settlers attracted to the West?

_____

_____

_____

Name _____ Class _____ Date _____

Focus Question: How were the civil rights of certain groups in America undermined during the years after Reconstruction?

Record the ways in which different groups challenged Reconstruction.

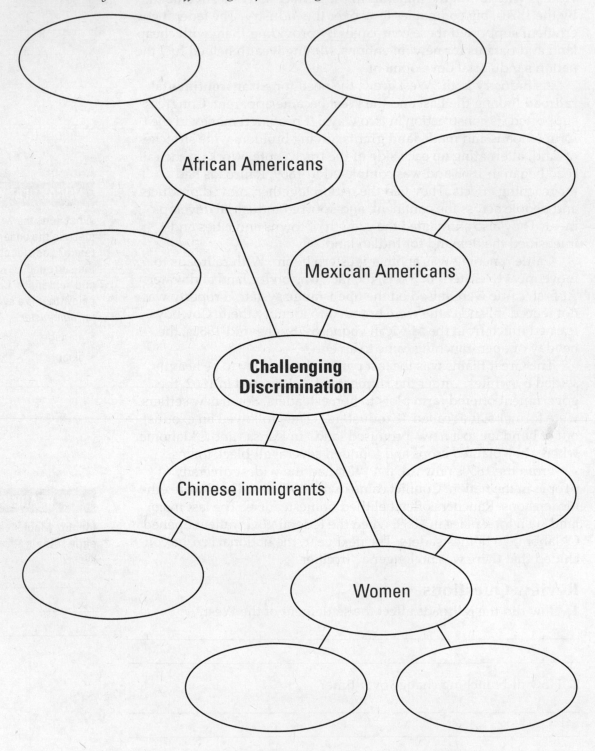

Name _____ Class _____ Date _____

Section Summary
SEGREGATION AND SOCIAL TENSIONS

After federal troops were removed from the South, southern states enacted **Jim Crow laws** that segregated blacks and whites. There were Jim Crow railroad cars, cemeteries, and restaurants, among other things. The Supreme Court case *Plessy* v. *Ferguson* declared these laws constitutional as long as states maintained "separate but equal" facilities. In reality, facilities were rarely equal.

Southern states exploited a number of African Americans by passing restrictive measures that disqualified many of them as voters. They enacted a **poll tax,** requiring voters to pay a tax to vote. Voters also had to pass **literacy tests.**

Even during the darkest days of Jim Crow, African Americans refused to accept their status as second-class citizens. They established black newspapers, women's clubs, fraternal organizations, schools and colleges, and political associations with the goal of securing their freedom. Former slave **Ida B. Wells** published the newspaper *Free Speech.* She wrote articles condemning the treatment of blacks and criticizing lynching. **Booker T. Washington** argued that African Americans needed to accommodate themselves to segregation, build up economic resources, and establish reputations as hardworking and honest citizens. **W.E.B. Du Bois** criticized Washington and argued that blacks should demand full and immediate equality.

Chinese immigrants also faced racial prejudice. Congress passed the Chinese Exclusion Act, prohibiting Chinese laborers from entering the country. Chinese migrants turned to the federal courts. In 1898, the Supreme Court ruled that individuals of Chinese descent who were born in America could not be stripped of their citizenship.

Mexican Americans also struggled against discrimination. Despite guaranteed property rights, many Mexicans lost their lands after the Mexican-American War because they were unable to prove ownership. In the late 1880s and early 1890s, **Las Gorras Blancas** (the White Caps) fought back by engaging in guerrilla warfare against the railroads and large ranchers.

Women continued to fight for the right to vote, to own property, and to receive an education. Although women failed to gain the vote, the number of women attending college jumped dramatically.

Review Questions

1. Describe actions southern states took to limit the rights of African Americans.

_____

_____

2. How did African Americans respond to segregation?

_____

_____

READING CHECK

What act prohibited Chinese workers from entering the United States?

_____

_____

_____

VOCABULARY STRATEGY

What does the word *exploited* mean in the underlined sentence? Circle any words or phrases in the surrounding sentences that help you figure out what *exploited* means.

_____

_____

_____

READING SKILL

Summarize Booker T. Washington and W.E.B. Du Bois had different responses to discrimination. Describe those responses.

_____

_____

_____

Name _____ Class _____ Date _____

Focus Question: Why did the political structure change during the Gilded Age?

As you read, describe the issues that dominated national politics in the 1870s and 1880s.

I. Politics and Economics

   A. Political Stalemate

   B. Corruption in Politics

      1. _____

      2. _____

      3. _____

   C. _____

      1. _____

      2. _____

         a. _____

         b. _____

CHAPTER 7 SECTION 2

Section Summary
POLITICAL AND ECONOMIC CHALLENGES

Inaction and political corruption characterized politics during the Gilded Age. Neither the Democrats nor the Republicans controlled the White House and both houses of Congress for more than two years in a row, making it difficult to pass new laws. Presidents during this era seemed weak and lacked integrity.

Political parties reached into nearly every ward and precinct in every city. Under the **spoils system,** politicians gave government jobs to loyal party workers without consideration of their qualifications. Government officials could and did use federal contracts to convince people to vote for their candidates.

A number of prominent figures promoted reforming the **civil service** system, a system that includes federal jobs in the executive branch. Under a reformed civil service, government workers would be offered jobs based on their expertise and keep those jobs regardless of which political party won the election. After President James Garfield was assassinated by a citizen who felt cheated out of a job, Vice President Chester Arthur signed the **Pendleton Civil Service Act** in 1883. This act established a civil service commission. The commission wrote an exam that all who sought government employment had to take before being hired. Getting a job was based on how well one did on the exam, not on one's political affiliation and connections.

Two economic issues created a political divide during the Gilded Age: the tariff and the monetary policy. Republicans favored a high tariff, arguing that it would promote job growth and allow American industry to grow. Democrats believed that high tariffs would raise prices and make it harder for American farmers to sell their goods abroad.

Disagreement flared over the **gold standard,** the use of gold as the basis of the nation's currency. Bankers and those in international trade feared that the use of silver for money would undermine the economy. Farmers argued that the rejection of silver money would lead to declining prices and financial ruin. Congress passed the Coinage Act of 1873, which ended the minting of silver coins, but after protest, it authorized minting of silver dollars.

Review Questions

1. How did the spoils system create government corruption?

_____

_____

2. Discuss how the civil service system was reformed after the assassination of President Garfield.

_____

_____

READING CHECK

What is the term for the use of gold as a nation's currency?

_____

_____

_____

VOCABULARY STRATEGY

What does the word *integrity* mean in the underlined sentence? The word "weak" earlier in the sentence has a negative meaning. Use this clue to help you figure out the meaning of *integrity.*

_____

_____

_____

READING SKILL

Identify Main Ideas Discuss two economic issues that were important to politics during the Gilded Age.

_____

_____

_____

Name _____ Class _____ Date _____

Note Taking Study Guide
FARMERS AND POPULISM

Focus Question: What led to the rise of the Populist movement, and what effect did it have?

As you read, list the reasons that farmers in the South and West felt the need to organize and the effects of their effort.

Causes	Effects
• Falling prices	•
•	
	•
•	
	•
•	
	•
•	
	•
•	

Event

Farmers organize.

CHAPTER 7 SECTION 3 — Section Summary
FARMERS AND POPULISM

Between 1870 and 1895, farm prices fell sharply. At the same time, the cost of doing business increased. Many farmers mortgaged their farms to survive. Farmers blamed big business, especially the railroads and banks, for their problems. They believed that railroads charged whatever rates they wanted and that banks set interest rates too high.

In 1867, **Oliver H. Kelley,** a Minnesota farmer and businessman, organized the **Grange,** an organization of farmers that grew to nearly a million members. <u>It was one of a network of organizations created to solve farmers' problems.</u> The Grange provided education and called for the regulation of railroad and grain elevator rates. Grangers also prompted the federal government to establish the Interstate Commerce Commission (ICC) to oversee interstate transportation.

Farmers' Alliances took up the call for reform in the late 1870s. They formed cooperatives to collectively sell crops and called on the federal government to establish "sub-treasuries," or postal banks, to provide farmers with low-interest loans.

The spread of the Farmers' Alliances culminated with the creation of the **Populist Party,** or People's Party, in 1892. The party grew rapidly, putting pressure on the two major political parties to consider their demands. They called for the coinage of silver, or "free silver," to fight low prices. To combat high costs, they demanded government ownership of railroads. In the 1892 election, the Populists elected several governors and senators, and ten congressmen. Their presidential candidate received more than one million votes.

Following this success, Populists were forced to decide whether to nominate their own presidential candidate or to endorse Democratic Party nominee **William Jennings Bryan** for the 1896 election. They chose to endorse Bryan, who supported many Populist proposals.

Bryan lost the election to Republican candidate **William McKinley,** partly because his emphasis on monetary reform, especially free silver, did not appeal to urban workers. The Populist decision to endorse Bryan weakened the party at the local and state levels. The party never recovered, and by the early 1900s, it had disappeared as a viable alternative to the two major political parties.

Review Questions

1. What did the Populist Party hope to achieve?

_____

_____

2. Describe why the Populist Party waned in the late 1890s.

_____

_____

READING CHECK

What candidate did Populists endorse in the 1896 presidential election?

_____

_____

_____

VOCABULARY STRATEGY

Find the word *network* in the underlined sentence. Eliminate the word from the sentence and read it again. What word might you use in place of *network*? Use this strategy to help you figure out the meaning of *network*.

_____

_____

_____

READING SKILL

Identify Causes and Effects
Describe the problems that led farmers to create groups such as the Grange.

_____

_____

_____

Name _____ Class _____ Date _____

Focus Question: What areas did Progressives think were in need of the greatest reform?

Fill in the chart below with details about Progressivism.

Progressivism

Problems	Muckrakers	Reforms
• Industrial hazards	• Exposed conditions	• Factory laws
•	•	•
•	•	•
•	•	•
•	•	•
•	•	•
•	•	•
		•
		•
		•
		•

CHAPTER 8 SECTION 1

Section Summary
THE DRIVE FOR REFORM

Industrialization, urbanization, and immigration brought many benefits to America, but they also produced challenging social problems. A movement called **Progressivism** arose in the 1890s to tackle these problems. Journalists whose stories dramatized the need for reform were called **muckrakers.** One leading muckraker was **Lincoln Steffens,** a magazine editor who published stories about political corruption. Another was **Jacob Riis,** a photographer whose pictures revealed life in urban slums. Novelist Frank Norris showed how the Southern Pacific Railroad kept a stranglehold on California farmers in *The Octopus.* Upton Sinclair's novel *The Jungle* revealed the unsafe and unsanitary conditions of Chicago meatpacking plants.

The work of the muckrakers increased popular support for Progressivism and helped the Progressives bring about reforms. Laws were passed to end child labor and break up monopolies and trusts. After a fire at a garment factory killed nearly 150 workers, Progressives were able to get laws passed to protect worker safety.

Many reformers thought that Christianity should be the basis of social reform. These followers of the **Social Gospel** believed that society would improve if people followed the Bible's teachings about charity and justice. One form of charity was the **settlement house,** which offered services for the poor such as child care and classes in English. Hull House in Chicago was a famous settlement house founded by **Jane Addams.** Her work inspired others to help solve the problems of the urban poor by becoming social workers.

In order to reform politics and remove corrupt governments, Progressives pushed for a number of new laws. <u>Dynamic leaders such as Governor Robert La Follette of Wisconsin created tools to limit the power of political bosses and business interests.</u> Reformers created the **direct primary** so citizens, not political bosses, could select nominees for upcoming elections. The **initiative** gave people the power to put a proposed new law directly on the ballot. The **referendum** allowed citizens to approve or reject laws passed by a legislature. The **recall** gave voters the power to remove elected officials from office before their terms ended. These reforms brought about by Progressives continue to affect society today.

Review Questions

1. Why were muckrakers important to Progressivism?

_____

_____

2. How did settlement houses help the poor?

_____

_____

READING CHECK

What were two examples of political reform?

_____

_____

_____

VOCABULARY STRATEGY

What does the word *dynamic* mean in the underlined sentence? Circle the words in the underlined sentence that could help you learn what *dynamic* means. Think about what kind of leader it would take to be a reformer.

_____

_____

_____

READING SKILL

Identify Details List four muckrakers whose work in the 1890s helped increase the public's awareness about social and political problems, and describe their work.

_____

_____

Note Taking Study Guide

CHAPTER 8 SECTION 2

WOMEN MAKE PROGRESS

Focus Question: How did women of the Progressive Era make progress and win the right to vote?

As you read this section, complete the outline below to capture the main ideas.

I. Women Expand Reforms

    A. Hardships for women

        1. _____

        2. _____

    B. _____

        1. _____

        2. _____

    C. _____

        1. _____

        2. _____

        3. _____

II. _____

    A. _____

        1. _____

        2. _____

    B. _____

        1. _____

        2. _____

    C. _____

        1. _____

        2. _____

Name _____ Class _____ Date _____

In the early 1900s, a growing number of women sought to do more than fulfill their roles as wives and mothers. Many went to college to prepare for careers in teaching and nursing. Women had already won a shorter workday, but reformers saw the need for more changes. **Florence Kelley** believed that unfair prices for household goods hurt women and their families, so she helped found the **National Consumers League (NCL).** The NCL labeled products made in safe workplaces. The NCL also asked the government to improve food and workplace safety and assist the unemployed.

Women also sought changes in the home. With the **temperance movement,** led by the Women's Christian Temperance Union (WCTU), women tried to reduce or end the consumption of alcohol. Members of the WCTU blamed alcohol for some men's abuse and neglect of their families. **Margaret Sanger** sought a different change. She thought that family life and women's health would improve if mothers had fewer children. Sanger opened the nation's first birth-control clinic. **Ida B. Wells** established the National Association of Colored Women, which helped African American families by providing childcare and education.

One of Progressivism's boldest goals was **suffrage**—the right to vote—for women. This fight was started in the 1860s but was reenergized by **Carrie Chapman Catt** in the 1890s. Catt toured the country encouraging women to join the **National American Woman Suffrage Association (NAWSA).** This group lobbied Congress for the right to vote and used the referendum process to try to get women the vote in individual states. <u>By 1918, this strategy had helped women get the vote in several states.</u> **Alice Paul** was more vocal in her efforts. In 1917, she formed the National Woman's Party (NWP), which staged protest marches and hunger strikes and even picketed the White House to demand the right to vote. When the United States entered World War I in 1917, the NAWSA supported the war effort. Its actions and those of the NWP convinced a growing number of legislators to support a woman suffrage amendment. This reform became official in 1920 as the **Nineteenth Amendment.** Women finally had the right to vote for President.

Review Questions

1. Why did many women want to end the drinking of alcohol?

_____

_____

2. What methods did reformers use to fight for women's suffrage?

_____

_____

READING CHECK

What is the Nineteenth Amendment?

_____

_____

VOCABULARY STRATEGY

What does the word *strategy* mean in the underlined sentence? What clues can you find in the surrounding words, phrases, or sentences? Circle the words in the underlined sentence that could help you learn what *strategy* means.

_____

_____

_____

READING SKILL

Identify Main Ideas What goal did Margaret Sanger, Ida B. Wells, and Florence Kelley share?

_____

_____

Name _____ Class _____ Date _____

CHAPTER 8 SECTION 3

Note Taking Study Guide
THE STRUGGLE AGAINST DISCRIMINATION

Focus Question: What steps did minorities take to combat social problems and discrimination?

Outline the section's main ideas and details.

I. The Struggle Against Discrimination

   A. _____

      1. _____

      2. _____

      3. _____

      4. _____

   B. _____

      1. _____

      2. _____

      3. _____

   C. _____

      1. _____

      2. _____

      3. _____

      4. _____

CHAPTER 8 SECTION 3

Section Summary
THE STRUGGLE AGAINST DISCRIMINATION

The Progressive Era was not so progressive for nonwhite and immigrant Americans. Most Progressives were white Anglo-Saxon Protestant reformers who were indifferent or hostile to minorities.

Settlement houses and other civic groups played a big role in the **Americanization** efforts of many Progressives. Americanization occurred when Progressives encouraged everyone to follow white, middle-class ways of life.

Many Progressives shared the same prejudices against nonwhites as other Americans. They agreed with so-called scientific theories that said that dark-skinned peoples had less intelligence than whites. They also supported segregation, or separation of the races, and laws to limit minority voting.

African American reformers responded in different ways to formal segregation and discrimination. For example, **Booker T. Washington** told blacks that the best way to win their rights was to be patient and to earn the respect of white Americans. **W.E.B. Du Bois,** on the other hand, said that blacks should demand immediately all the rights guaranteed by the Constitution.

W.E.B. Du Bois was a member of the **Niagara Movement,** a group that called for rapid progress and more education for blacks. After a race riot broke out in Illinois, its members joined with white reformers to form the **National Association for the Advancement of Colored People (NAACP).** The NAACP planned to use the court system to fight for the civil rights of African Americans, including the right to vote. The efforts of the NAACP mostly helped middle-class blacks, but the **Urban League** focused on poorer urban workers. It helped families buy clothes and books and helped factory workers and maids find jobs.

African Americans were not alone in seeking their rights. Individuals and organizations of diverse ethnic groups spoke out against injustice and created self-help agencies. Jews in New York City formed the **Anti-Defamation League** to defend themselves against verbal attacks and false statements. Mexican Americans in several states formed **mutualistas,** groups that gave loans and provided legal assistance to the poor.

Review Questions

1. Why did Progressives not fight for the civil rights of minorities?

_____

_____

2. How did the Urban League differ from the NAACP?

_____

_____

READING CHECK

Who organized the Anti-Defamation League?

_____

_____

_____

VOCABULARY STRATEGY

What does the word *so-called* mean in the underlined sentence? Two synonyms for *so-called* are *supposed* and *presumed.* Use the meanings of the synonyms to help you determine the meaning of *so-called.*

_____

_____

_____

READING SKILL

Main Idea and Details How did Booker T. Washington differ from W.E.B. Du Bois in his approach to civil rights?

_____

_____

_____

Name _____ Class _____ Date _____

Focus Question: What did Roosevelt think government should do for citizens?

A. *As you read this section, use the concept web below to record the main ideas.*

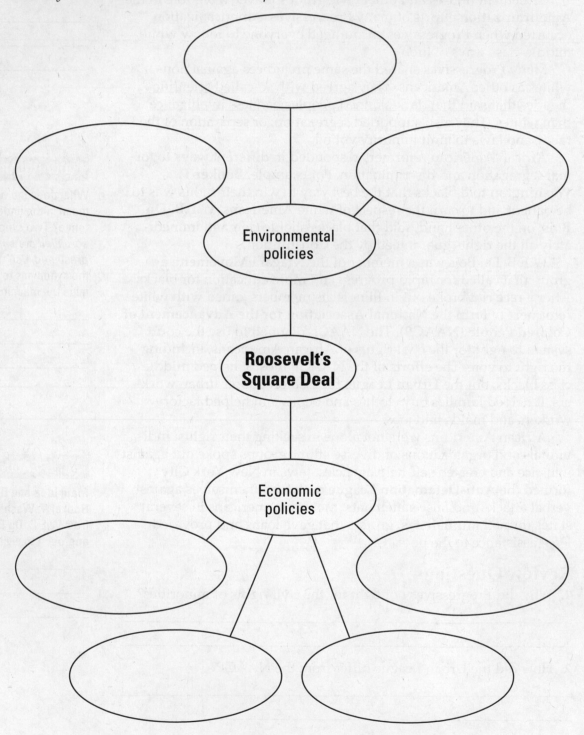

CHAPTER 8 SECTION 4

Note Taking Study Guide
ROOSEVELT'S SQUARE DEAL

Focus Question: What did Roosevelt think government should do for citizens?

B. *As you read, fill in the Venn diagram with similarities and differences between Roosevelt and Taft.*

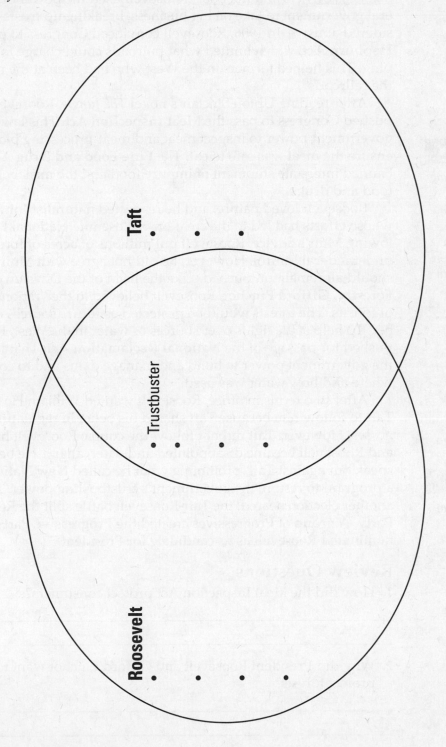

Taft

•   •   •

Trustbuster

•   •   •   •

Roosevelt

•   •   •   •

CHAPTER

8

SECTION 4

Section Summary
ROOSEVELT'S SQUARE DEAL

READING CHECK

What was New Nationalism?

_____

_____

_____

VOCABULARY STRATEGY

What does the word *dominating* mean in the underlined sentence? What clues can you find in the surrounding words, phrases, or sentences? Circle the words in the underlined sentence that could help you learn what *dominating* means.

_____

_____

_____

READING SKILL

Identify Main Ideas How were the Square Deal and the New Nationalism programs similar?

_____

_____

_____

Theodore Roosevelt was a war hero, seasoned politician, and a dedicated reformer when he became President in 1901. <u>He quickly pushed Congress to approve the Square Deal, a program of reform aimed at stopping the wealthy and powerful from dominating small business owners and the poor.</u> Roosevelt used the power of the federal government to take on big business, breaking up trusts he considered abusive. In 1906, Roosevelt convinced Congress to pass the **Hepburn Act,** which limited what railroads could charge for shipping. This helped farmers in the West who had been at the mercy of the railroads.

After reading Upton Sinclair's novel *The Jungle,* Roosevelt pushed Congress to pass the **Meat Inspection Act.** This law gave the government power to inspect meat and meat-processing plants to ensure the meat was safe to eat. The **Pure Food and Drug Act** banned interstate shipment of impure food and the mislabeling of food and drugs.

Roosevelt loved nature, and he respected naturalist **John Muir,** whose efforts had led to the creation of Yosemite National Park. Following Muir's advice, Roosevelt put millions of acres of forests under federal control. However, he did not agree with Muir that it should all remain untouched. Like the head of the Division of Forestry, **Gifford Pinchot,** Roosevelt believed in the "rational use" of forests. The forests would be protected as future sources of lumber. To help settle fights over sources of water in the West, Roosevelt pushed for passage of the **National Reclamation Act.** That law gave the government power to build and manage dams and to control where and how water was used.

After two terms in office, Roosevelt wanted William Howard Taft to follow him because Taft shared his belief in regulating businesses. However, Taft did not follow the course Roosevelt had set, and Roosevelt became disappointed and, later, angry. He began to speak out against Taft, promoting what he called **New Nationalism,** a program to restore the government's trustbusting power. As another election neared, the Taft-Roosevelt battle split the Republican Party. A group of Progressives created the **Progressive Party** and nominated Roosevelt as its candidate for President.

Review Questions

1. How did the Meat Inspection Act protect consumers?

_____

_____

2. Why did President Roosevelt and Gifford Pinchot want to protect forests?

_____

_____

Name _____ Class _____ Date _____

Note Taking Study Guide
WILSON'S NEW FREEDOM

Focus Question: What steps did Wilson take to increase the government's role in the economy?

As you read this section, fill in the concept web below to record details from the section.

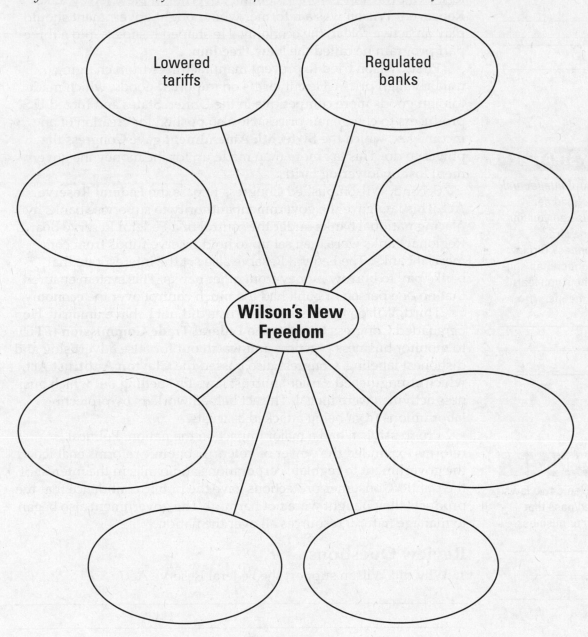

CHAPTER 8 SECTION 5

Section Summary
WILSON'S NEW FREEDOM

What did Wilson call his plan for reform?

_____

_____

_____

What does the word *intellectual* mean in the underlined sentence? What clues can you find in the surrounding words, phrases, or sentences? Circle the words in the underlined sentence that could help you learn what *intellectual* means.

_____

_____

_____

Identify Details Name two laws that Wilson helped pass that reformed banking or business.

_____

_____

_____

During the 1912 election, Roosevelt and Taft split the Republican Party vote, allowing Democrat **Woodrow Wilson** to win the election. Wilson was an intellectual man from Virginia who had taught college as a professor before becoming governor of New Jersey. Like Roosevelt, Wilson was a reformer who thought government should play an active role in the economy. He shaped his ideas into a three-part program he called the **New Freedom.**

First, Wilson tried to prevent manufacturers from charging unfairly high prices. He cut tariffs on imported goods, which made foreign goods more competitive in the United States and forced U.S. producers to charge fair prices. He also pushed for creation of an income tax, which the **Sixteenth Amendment** gave Congress the power to do. This tax more than made up for the money the government lost by lowering tariffs.

Second, Wilson pushed Congress to pass the **Federal Reserve Act.** This law gave the government authority to supervise banks by placing national banks under the control of a Federal Reserve Board. Regional banks were then set up to hold reserve funds from commercial banks. The Federal Reserve also set the interest rate that banks pay to borrow money from other banks. This system ensured that no one person or bank had too much control over the economy.

Third, Wilson made sure that trusts did not behave unfairly. He persuaded Congress to create the **Federal Trade Commission (FTC)** to monitor business practices and watch out for false advertising and dishonest labeling. Congress also passed the **Clayton Antitrust Act,** which strengthened earlier antitrust laws by spelling out which business activities were illegal. The act helped workers by protecting labor unions from being attacked as trusts.

Progressivism had a major impact on the nation. Political reforms expanded the power of voters. Economic reforms enabled the government to regulate corporations and banks in the interest of the public. Consumer protections gave the public confidence that the products they bought were not harmful. The government also began to manage natural resources all over the nation.

Review Questions

1. Why did Wilson support the Federal Reserve Act?

_____

_____

2. What were three ways Wilson wanted to regulate the economy?

_____

_____

Focus Question: How and why did the United States take a more active role in world affairs?

As you read, fill in the concept web below with the key events that marked America's first steps toward world power.

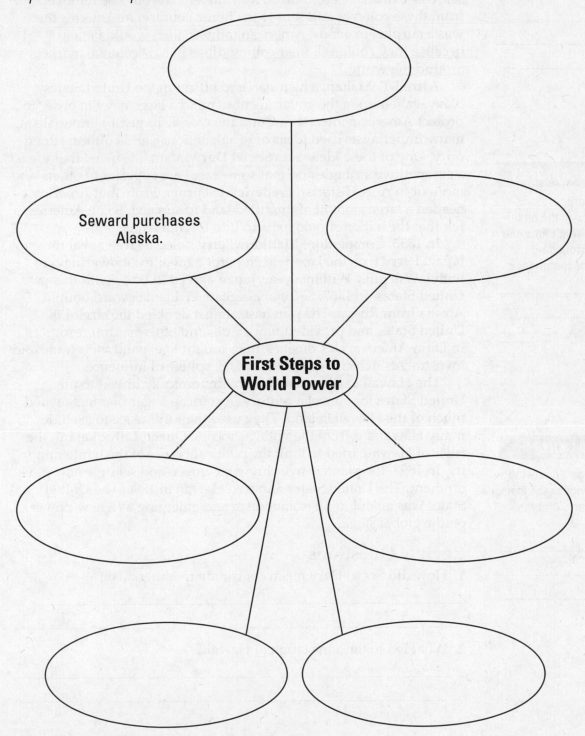

Seward purchases Alaska.

First Steps to World Power

Name _____ Class _____ Date _____

READING CHECK

How did Commodore Matthew Perry win the Japanese emperor's favor?

_____

_____

_____

VOCABULARY STRATEGY

What does the word *commodities* mean in the underlined sentence? What clues can you find in the surrounding words, phrases, or sentences?

_____

_____

_____

READING SKILL

Identify Main Ideas Locate the sentence that identifies the main idea of the summary. Write the sentence below.

_____

_____

_____

During the late 1800s, the United States began to acquire influence and territory outside of its continental borders. It pursued a policy of **imperialism,** or the use of economic, political, and military control over weaker territories. Many imperialist nations wanted colonies to serve as **extractive economies.** Raw materials would be removed from these colonies and sent to the home country. In America there was a surplus of goods. <u>American industrialists would benefit because they could sell their commodities in new colonial markets around the world.</u>

    Alfred T. Mahan, a historian and officer in the United States Navy, called upon the government to build a large navy in order to protect American interests around the world. To justify imperialism, many imperialists used ideas of racial, national, and cultural superiority. One of these ideas was **Social Darwinism,** the belief that life is a competitive struggle and that some races are superior to others and more fit to rule. Historian **Frederick J. Turner** wrote that America needed a large amount of unsettled land to succeed. Some Americans felt that the nation should expand into foreign lands.

    In 1853, Commodore **Matthew Perry** sailed a large naval force to Japan. Perry won the Japanese emperor's favor by showering him with lavish gifts. Within a year, Japan agreed to trade with the United States. In 1867, Secretary of State William Seward bought Alaska from Russia. The purchase almost doubled the size of the United States and provided timber, oil, and other natural resources. In Latin America, U.S. businessmen sought to expand their trade and investments, which expanded the U.S. sphere of influence.

    The Hawaiian Islands had been economically linked to the United States for almost a century. American sugar planters owned much of the Hawaiian land. They used their influence to exclude many Hawaiians from the voting process. **Queen Liliuokalani,** the ruler of Hawaii, tried to limit the political power of the white minority. In 1893, the planters overthrew the queen and set up a new government. The United States annexed Hawaii in 1898. The United States was abandoning isolationism and emerging as a new power on the global stage.

Review Questions

1. How did Social Darwinism contribute to imperialism?

_____

_____

2. What led to the annexation of Hawaii?

_____

_____

Name _____ Class _____ Date _____

CHAPTER 9 SECTION 2

Note Taking Study Guide
THE SPANISH-AMERICAN WAR

Focus Question: What were the causes and effects of the Spanish-American War?

As you read, note the causes, key events, and effects of the Spanish-American War.

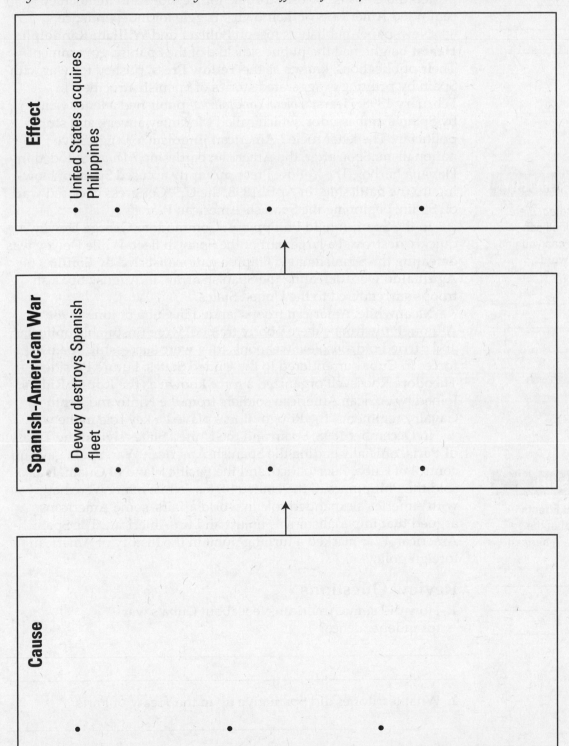

Effect

- United States acquires Philippines
- •
- •
- •

Spanish-American War

- Dewey destroys Spanish fleet
- •
- •
- •

Cause

- •
- •
- •

Name _____ Class _____ Date _____

What was the Yellow Press?

_____

_____

_____

What does the word *obsolete* mean in the underlined sentence? What clues can you find in the surrounding words, phrases, or sentences?

_____

_____

_____

Identify Causes and Effects
What was the effect of the Yellow Press on the American public?

_____

_____

_____

At the end of the nineteenth century, tensions were rising between Spain and its colony in Cuba. Cuban patriot **José Martí** launched a war for independence from Spain in 1895. Many Americans supported the Cubans, whose struggle for freedom and democracy reminded Americans of their own struggle for independence.

Newspaper publishers Joseph Pulitzer and **William Randolph Hearst** heightened the public's dislike of the Spanish government. Their publications, known as the **Yellow Press,** pushed for war with Spain by printing exaggerated stories of Spanish atrocities. In February 1898, Hearst's *New York Journal* published a letter written by Spain's ambassador, which called McKinley a weak and stupid politician. The letter fueled American **jingoism,** or aggressive nationalism. Soon after, the American battleship *Maine* exploded in Havana harbor. The Yellow Press promptly accused Spain of blowing up the battleship. In April 1898, the U.S. Congress declared war on Spain, beginning the Spanish-American War.

In the Spanish-held Philippines, Commodore **George Dewey** quickly destroyed a large part of the Spanish fleet. While Dewey was defeating the Spanish navy, Filipino nationalists led by **Emilio Aguinaldo** were defeating the Spanish army. In August, Spanish troops surrendered to the United States.

Meanwhile, American troops landed in Cuba in June 1898. <u>Although the troops were poorly trained, wore unsuitable uniforms, and carried old, obsolete weapons, they were successful.</u> Spanish forces in Cuba surrendered to the United States. Future President Theodore Roosevelt organized a force known as the **Rough Riders.** Joined by African American soldiers from the Ninth and Tenth Cavalry regiments, the Rough Riders played a key role in the war.

In December 1898, Spain and the United States signed the **Treaty of Paris,** officially ending the Spanish-American War. Spain gave up control of Cuba, Puerto Rico, and the Pacific island of Guam. It also sold the Philippines to the United States. While many were happy with America's expanded role in world affairs, some Americans argued that imperialism was unjust and un-American. The Spanish-American War marked a turning point in the history of American foreign policy.

Review Questions

1. How did some Americans feel about Cuba's war for independence?

_____

_____

2. What territories did Spain give up in the Treaty of Paris?

_____

_____

CHAPTER
9
SECTION 3

Note Taking Study Guide
THE UNITED STATES AND EAST ASIA

Focus Question: How did the United States extend its influence in Asia?

As you read, use the timeline to trace events and developments in East Asia that tested America's new global power.

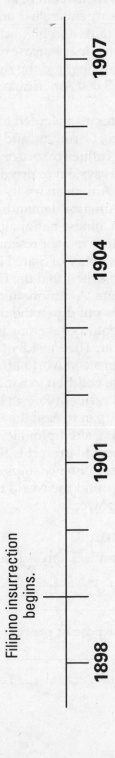

1907

1904

1901

Filipino insurrection begins.

1898

CHAPTER 9

SECTION 3

Section Summary

THE UNITED STATES AND EAST ASIA

During the Spanish-American War, Filipino nationalist Emilio Aguinaldo viewed America as an ally in the Filipino struggle for independence. However, when the United States kept possession of the Philippines after the war, Aguinaldo grew disillusioned. He helped organize an **insurrection,** or rebellion, against U.S. rule.

The Filipino insurgents relied on **guerrilla warfare** tactics, including surprise raids and hit-and-run attacks. In turn, the U.S. military used extraordinary measures to crush the rebellion. <u>The war in the Philippines highlighted the rigors of fighting against guerrilla insurgents.</u> Nearly 5,000 Americans and 200,000 Filipinos were killed in the fighting.

The United States also wanted to increase trade with China. By 1899, Britain, France, Germany, and Russia had carved China into distinct **spheres of influence,** or zones. Because the United States did not have a zone, this system of privileged access to Chinese markets threatened to limit American trade. U.S. Secretary of State **John Hay** made it clear that America demanded equal trade access.

In May 1900, a Chinese nationalist group launched the **Boxer Rebellion** in objection to the presence of foreigners. As the rebellion engulfed China, Secretary of State Hay reasserted America's **Open Door Policy,** which stated that the United States wanted free trade, not colonies, in China. A multinational force of European, American, and Japanese troops put down the uprising.

In 1905, President Roosevelt negotiated an end to the **Russo-Japanese War.** The President's intervention displayed America's growing role in world affairs. However, in 1906, the segregation of Japanese children in San Francisco schools drew Japan's immediate wrath. President Roosevelt negotiated a **"Gentlemen's Agreement"** with Japan to ease the tension.

While Roosevelt used diplomacy with Japan, he also promoted military preparedness to protect U.S. interests in Asia. In 1907, Roosevelt sent a force of navy ships, known as the **Great White Fleet,** on a cruise around the world to demonstrate America's increased military power.

VOCABULARY STRATEGY

What does the word *rigors* mean in the underlined sentence? What clues can you find in the surrounding words, phrases, or sentences?

_____

_____

_____

READING SKILL

Recognize Sequence Number the following events in chronological order.

_____ Great White Fleet sails

_____ China carved into spheres of influence

_____ Roosevelt negotiates "Gentlemen's Agreement"

Review Questions

1. What problem did U.S. forces face in the Philippines?

_____

_____

2. What was the purpose of proclaiming the Open Door Policy?

_____

_____

CHAPTER 9 SECTION 4

Note Taking Study Guide

THE UNITED STATES AND LATIN AMERICA

Focus Question: What actions did the United States take to achieve its goals in Latin America?

A. *Complete the table below to note how the United States dealt with Puerto Rico and Cuba.*

American Policy After Spanish-American War	
Puerto Rico	**Cuba**
• Foraker Act establishes civil government in 1900 • •	• • •

Name _____ Class _____ Date _____

Focus Question: What actions did the United States take to achieve its goals in Latin America?

B. *As you read, compare Wilson's moral diplomacy with the foreign policies of Roosevelt and Taft by completing the flowchart below.*

United States Foreign Policy

Roosevelt	Taft	Wilson
•	•	• "Moral diplomacy"
		•
•	•	
		•
• Supported rebellion in Panama		
•		•

CHAPTER 9 SECTION 4

Section Summary

THE UNITED STATES AND LATIN AMERICA

After the Spanish-American War, the United States assumed control of Puerto Rico and Cuba. In 1900, the U.S. Congress passed the **Foraker Act,** which established a civil government in Puerto Rico. Later, in 1917, Puerto Ricans gained more citizenship rights and greater control over their own legislature.

Before the United States Army withdrew from Cuba in 1902, Congress forced Cuba to add the **Platt Amendment** to its constitution. The amendment restricted the rights of newly independent Cubans, gave the United States the right to intervene in Cuba, and made Cuba a protectorate of the United States.

After assuming the presidency, Theodore Roosevelt promoted **"big stick" diplomacy,** which relied on a strong U.S. military to achieve America's goals. Roosevelt used this forceful approach to intimidate Colombia and gain control over the "Canal Zone" in Panama. America then built the **Panama Canal,** a waterway that connected the Atlantic and Pacific oceans.

In 1904, President Roosevelt announced the **Roosevelt Corollary,** which updated the Monroe Doctrine for an age of economic imperialism. The policy stated that the United States would serve as the policing power in Latin America and would restore order when necessary. Many Latin Americans resented America's role as the hemisphere's police force.

President William Howard Taft shared Roosevelt's basic foreign policy objectives. However, Taft stressed **"dollar diplomacy,"** which aimed to increase American investments throughout Central America and the Caribbean. In 1913, President Woodrow Wilson, who had criticized imperialism, promoted his policy of **"moral diplomacy."** Wilson promised that America would work to promote "human rights, national integrity, and opportunity."

Although he intended to take U.S. policy in a different direction, President Wilson nevertheless used the military on a number of occasions. During the Mexican Revolution, Wilson sent marines to help Venustiano Carranza, a reformer, to assume the presidency. Wilson also sent troops to capture **Francisco "Pancho" Villa,** whose raid into New Mexico left 18 Americans dead. America's triumph over Spain and U.S. actions in Asia and Latin America demonstrated that America had emerged as a global power.

Review Questions

1. What did "big stick" diplomacy rely on?

_____

_____

2. How was Wilson's foreign policy different from Roosevelt's?

_____

_____

READING CHECK

Why might Cubans have resented the Platt Amendment?

_____

_____

_____

VOCABULARY STRATEGY

What does the word *nevertheless* mean in the underlined sentence? Circle the words in the underlined passage that could help you learn what *nevertheless* means.

_____

_____

_____

READING SKILL

Identify Supporting Details
What details support the idea that Wilson did not always follow "moral diplomacy"?

_____

_____

_____

Note Taking Study Guide

FROM NEUTRALITY TO WAR

Focus Question: What caused World War I, and why did the United States enter the war?

As you read, identify the causes of World War I, the conditions facing soldiers, and the reasons for U.S. involvement.

World War I

Reasons for U.S. involvement

-
-
-
-

Nature of warfare

-
-
-

Causes of the war

-
-
-
-

CHAPTER 10 SECTION 1

Section Summary

FROM NEUTRALITY TO WAR

Although there had been no major wars, the 50 years before World War I were not tranquil. Nationalism renewed old grudges among countries. **Militarism,** or glorification of the military, eventually produced an arms race between Germany and Britain at sea and among Germany, France, and Russia on land.

In addition to strengthening their military power, European leaders prepared for war by forming alliances. Germany, Austria-Hungary, and Italy formed the Triple Alliance. Opposing them were France, Russia, and Great Britain, which formed the Triple Entente. In 1914, a Serbian youth assassinated **Francis Ferdinand,** the archduke of Austria-Hungary. War spread as European countries entered the fighting to help their allies. Russia came to the aid of Serbia against Austria. Germany declared war on Russia. France, Russia's ally, declared war on Germany. After Germany declared war on Belgium, Great Britain declared war on Germany. World War I had begun.

Although fighting went on in Eastern Europe, the Middle East, and other parts of the world, the **Western Front** in France became the critical battle front. German soldiers settled onto high ground, dug trenches, and fortified their position. The French and British then dug their own trenches. A stalemate developed and the war dragged on for years. New military technology, including machine guns and poison gas, led to millions of **casualties.**

As the war continued in Europe, President Woodrow Wilson called for Americans to remain impartial. However, the brutal German invasion of Belgium swayed American opinion against Germany. Americans also protested when a German submarine, or **U-boat,** sank the British passenger liner *Lusitania.*

In January 1917, German Foreign Minister Arthur Zimmermann sent a telegram to Mexico proposing an alliance between Germany and Mexico. The **Zimmermann note** was intercepted by the British, who gave it to American authorities. When the telegram was published, Americans were shocked by its contents. Next, Germany announced unrestricted submarine warfare against Britain. On April 6, 1917, the United States Congress declared war on Germany.

Review Questions

1. How did the alliances between European countries lead to war?

_____

_____

2. Why did the United States get involved in the war?

_____

_____

READING CHECK

Who was Francis Ferdinand?

_____

_____

_____

VOCABULARY BUILDER

What does the word *allies* mean in the underlined sentence? What clues can you find in the surrounding words, phrases, or sentences? Circle the words that could help you learn what *allies* means.

_____

_____

_____

READING SKILL

Identify Causes Identify the causes of World War I.

_____

_____

_____

CHAPTER 10 SECTION 2

Note Taking Study Guide
THE HOME FRONT

Focus Question: How did the war affect Americans at home?

As you read, summarize the key points made in the section in the chart below.

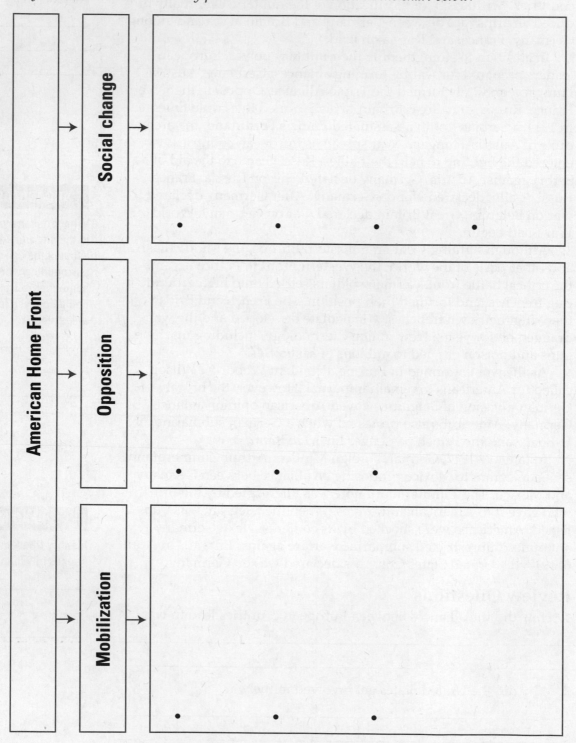

American Home Front

Social change
- •
- •
- •
- •

Opposition
- •
- •
- •

Mobilization
- •
- •
- •

CHAPTER 10 SECTION 2

Section Summary
THE HOME FRONT

When the United States entered World War I, its army was only a fraction of the size of European armies. To build the army, Congress passed the **Selective Service Act,** which authorized a draft of young men for military service in Europe.

While the Selective Service Commission raised an army, the War Industries Board (WIB), headed by **Bernard Baruch,** regulated all industries engaged in the war effort. <u>The WIB also urged Americans to conserve food as a patriotic gesture.</u> As head of the Food Administration, future U.S. President Herbert Hoover set high prices for food to encourage farmers to increase production.

In 1917, many Americans questioned U.S. involvement in the war. The **Committee on Public Information (CPI)** worked to convince the American public that the war effort was a just cause. **George Creel,** the director of the CPI, combined education and a widespread advertising campaign to "sell America."

Still, not all Americans favored America's entry into the war. German Americans and Irish Americans tended to oppose the Allies. Opposition also came from **conscientious objectors,** people whose moral or religious beliefs forbid them to fight in wars.

During the war, the U.S. government restricted individual rights. In June 1917, Congress passed the **Espionage Act,** which banned subversive newspapers, magazines, or printed materials. Congress further limited freedom of speech with the Sedition Act. In *Schenck* v. *United States* (1919), the Supreme Court ruled that there are times when the First Amendment protections on speech do not apply.

The war also brought substantial social changes. It created jobs for women while men were serving in the military and ushered in the Nineteenth Amendment, which gave women the right to vote. Meanwhile, a great movement of African Americans from the rural South to the industrial North was taking place. The **Great Migration** saw more than 1.2 million African Americans move to the North to escape racism and find better jobs. Many Mexicans also sought to improve their lives. Some crossed the border into the United States, where they looked for jobs. World War I had opened up new opportunities for women, African Americans, and Mexican Americans.

Review Questions

1. What was the purpose of the Committee on Public Information (CPI)?

_____

_____

2. Why did conscientious objectors oppose the war?

_____

_____

READING CHECK

Why did many African Americans move to the North during the Great Migration?

_____

_____

_____

VOCABULARY BUILDER

What does the word *conserve* mean in the underlined sentence? An antonym for *conserve* is *squander.* Use the antonym to help you figure out the meaning of *conserve.*

_____

_____

_____

READING SKILL

Summarize Summarize how the American government mobilized the public to support the war effort.

_____

_____

_____

CHAPTER 10 SECTION 3 — Note Taking Study Guide

WILSON, WAR, AND PEACE

Focus Question: How did Americans affect the end of World War I and its peace settlements?

A. *As you read, sequence the events leading to the end of World War I in the timeline below.*

Armistice ends war. — Nov. 1918

U-boat war intensifies. — March 1917

CHAPTER
10
SECTION 3

Note Taking Study Guide

WILSON, WAR, AND PEACE

Focus Question: How did Americans affect the end of World War I and its peace settlements?

B. *As you read, summarize Wilson's goals for peace and whether or not each goal was fulfilled.*

Wilson's Ideas for Peace	Decision Made at Paris Peace Conference
Peace without victory	Great Britain and France make Germany pay reparations.
Open diplomacy	
Freedom of seas and free trade	
Move toward ending colonialism	
Self-determination	
League of Nations	

Name _____ Class _____ Date _____

When the United States entered World War I in 1917, the conflict had become a deadly stalemate. Hoping to end the conflict before the Americans could make a difference, Germany renewed unrestricted submarine warfare. British and American **convoys** provided mutual safety by sending warships to protect the merchant ships. As a result, shipping losses from U-boat attacks fell sharply.

In November 1917, radical communists led by **Vladimir Lenin** gained control of Russia. Fighting stopped between Russia and Germany, which allowed Germany to launch an all-out offensive on the Western Front. American troops under the command of **John J. Pershing** helped stop the German offensive and launch successful counteroffensives. On November 11, 1918, Germany surrendered, officially ending World War I.

In what became known as the **Fourteen Points,** President Woodrow Wilson promoted openness, encouraged independence, and supported freedom. Wilson also advocated **self-determination,** or the right of people to choose their own form of government. Finally, he asked for a **League of Nations,** a world organization where countries could gather and peacefully resolve their quarrels.

In 1919, the victorious Allies held a peace conference in France. Although Wilson's hope for the League of Nations was fulfilled, the various peace treaties created almost as many problems as they solved. The other Allied leaders insisted that Germany make **reparations,** or payment for war damages. When the map of Europe was redrawn, national self-determination was violated many times.

In the United States, many people opposed the treaty. A handful of senators known as the **"irreconcilables"** believed that the United States should not get entangled in world organizations such as the League of Nations. A larger group of senators, led by **Henry Cabot Lodge** and known as the **"reservationists,"** was opposed to the treaty as it was written. Wilson and his opponents refused to put aside their differences and compromise, and the Senate did not ratify the treaty. Without full American support, the League of Nations proved unable to maintain peace among nations.

Review Questions

1. Describe the aims of the Fourteen Points.

_____

_____

2. How did convoys contribute to the success of the Allies?

_____

_____

Name _____ Class _____ Date _____

Focus Question: What political, economic, and social effects did World War I have on the United States?

As you read, identify and record the main ideas of this section in the concept web below.

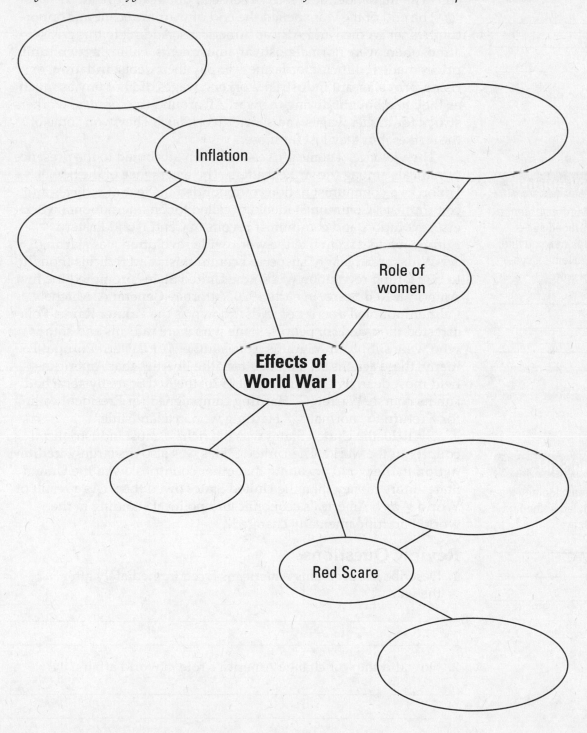

Inflation

Role of women

Effects of World War I

Red Scare

CHAPTER 10 SECTION 4

Section Summary
EFFECTS OF THE WAR

READING CHECK

READING CHECK

Why did Harding win the 1920 presidential election?

_____

_____

_____

VOCABULARY BUILDER

What does the word *emergence* mean in the underlined sentence? What clues can you find in the root word? Name a synonym for the root word.

_____

_____

_____

READING SKILL

Identify Main Ideas Identify the main factors that led to the first American Red Scare.

_____

_____

_____

World War I produced significant economic, social, political, and cultural changes in America. An **influenza** virus that killed millions worldwide made the movement from war to peace even more difficult. The flu pandemic created a sense of doom and dread.

The end of the war spelled the end of wartime economic opportunities for women and African Americans. Adding to this crisis atmosphere were normal postwar adjustments. Falling agricultural prices made it difficult for farmers to pay their debts. **Inflation,** or rising prices, meant industrial workers' wages did not buy as much as they had bought during the war. All around the country, workers struck for higher wages and shorter workdays. They won some of the strikes, but they lost far more.

The violence of some strikes was often attributed to the presence of radicals among the strike leaders. <u>The emergence of the Soviet Union as a communist nation compounded the fear of radicals and communists.</u> Communist ideology called for an international workers' revolution, and communist revolts in Central and Eastern Europe made it seem like the worldwide revolution was starting.

Widespread fear of suspected communists and radicals thought to be plotting revolution within the United States prompted the first American **Red Scare.** In early 1920, Attorney General A. Mitchell Palmer mounted a series of raids, known as the **Palmer Raids.** Police arrested thousands of people, some who were radicals and some who were simply immigrants from southern or Eastern Europe. To many, these actions seemed to attack the liberties that Americans held most dear. By the summer of 1920, the Red Scare hysteria had run its course. **Warren G. Harding** campaigned for President calling for a return to "normalcy." Harding won in a landslide.

By 1920, the United States was the richest, most industrialized country in the world. The United States was also the largest **creditor nation** in the world, meaning that other countries owed the United States more money than the United States owed them. As a result of World War I, America's economic and political standing in the world had fundamentally changed.

Review Questions

1. Describe the problems Americans faced immediately after the war.

_____

_____

2. How did the war change America's role in world affairs?

_____

_____

Name _____ Class _____ Date _____

Note Taking Study Guide
A BOOMING ECONOMY

Focus Question: How did the booming economy of the 1920s lead to changes in American life?

As you read, note specific examples that support the idea that the economy changed during the 1920s.

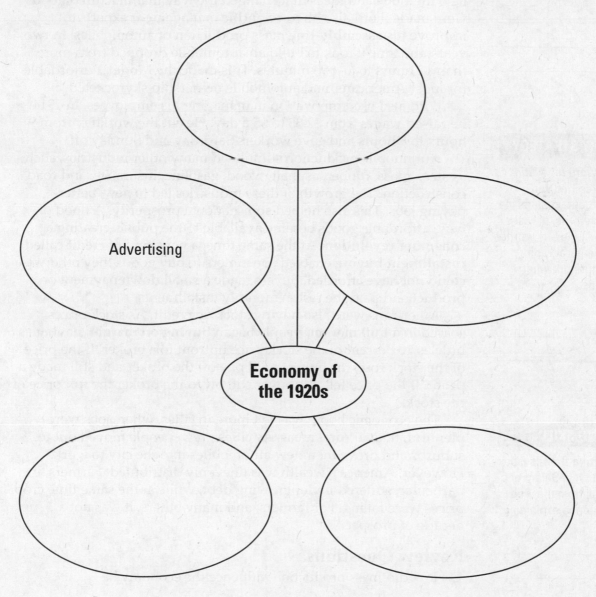

Advertising

Economy of
the 1920s

CHAPTER 11 SECTION 1

Section Summary
A BOOMING ECONOMY

READING CHECK

READING CHECK

What industries were helped by the increase in automobile ownership?

_____

_____

_____

VOCABULARY STRATEGY

What does the word *innovation* mean in the underlined sentence? Look for context clues in the surrounding words, phrases, and sentences. Circle any words or phrases in the paragraph that help you figure out what *innovation* means.

_____

_____

_____

READING SKILL

Identify Supporting Details Look at your concept web. Select one supporting detail from the web and write a sentence explaining this detail.

_____

_____

_____

During the 1920s, revolutionary **mass-production** techniques enabled American workers to produce more goods in less time. Because of this, the economy boomed. The automobile industry played a major role in the boom. Carmaker **Henry Ford** introduced new methods and ideas that changed the way manufactured goods were made. Ford also hired **scientific management** experts to improve his **assembly-line** mass production of automobiles. In two years, the time it took to build an automobile dropped from more than 12 hours to just 90 minutes. This made the **Model T** affordable for most Americans, and automobile ownership skyrocketed.

Ford also used innovation in managing his employees. In 1914, he raised wages from $2.35 to $5 a day. He cut the workday from 9 hours to 8 hours and gave workers Saturday and Sunday off.

Automobile production stimulated many other industries, such as steel, glass, rubber, asphalt, wood, gasoline, insurance, and road construction. The growth of these industries led to new, better-paying jobs. This also helped spur national prosperity. A flood of new, affordable goods became available to the public, creating a **consumer revolution.** At the same time, a new kind of credit called **installment buying** enabled consumers to buy goods they otherwise could not have afforded. Buyers made a small down payment on a product and paid the rest in monthly installments.

Americans were also buying stock on credit. As stock prices soared in a **bull market,** people began **buying on margin,** paying as little as 10 percent of the stock price upfront to a broker. If the price of the stock rose, the buyer could pay off the broker and still made a profit. If the price fell, the buyer still owed the broker the full price of the stock.

The economic boom was felt more in cities, where jobs were plentiful, than in rural areas. As cities grew, people moved out to suburbs and drove their new automobiles into the city to work. However, America's wealth was unevenly distributed. Farmers, in particular, suffered under growing debt, while at the same time crop prices were falling. For farmers, and many others, it was not a decade of prosperity.

Review Questions

1. How did mass production influence the economy?

_____

_____

2. What was installment buying?

_____

_____

CHAPTER 11
SECTION 2

Note Taking Study Guide

THE BUSINESS OF GOVERNMENT

Focus Question: How did domestic and foreign policy change direction under Harding and Coolidge?

As you read, note similarities and differences between the characters and policies of Presidents Harding and Coolidge.

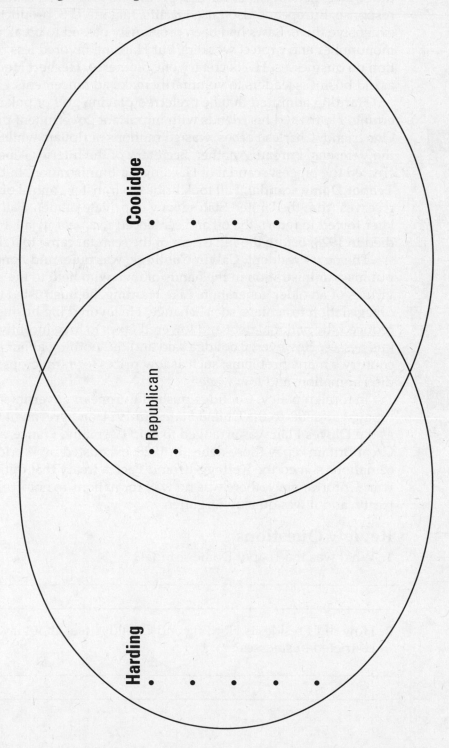

Coolidge

· · · · ·

Republican

· · ·

Harding

· · · · ·

Name _____ Class _____ Date _____

READING CHECK

What was the purpose of the Kellogg-Briand Pact?

_____

_____

_____

VOCABULARY STRATEGY

Find the word *incentives* in the underlined sentence. Money, rewards, and praise are sometimes used as incentives. What is the meaning of *incentives?*

_____

_____

_____

READING SKILL

Compare and Contrast Look at the diagram comparing similarities and differences between Presidents Harding and Coolidge. How did their differences influence their presidencies?

_____

_____

_____

In 1920, fun-loving Warren G. Harding was elected President. Preferring a laissez-faire approach to business, Harding named banker **Andrew Mellon** as Secretary of the Treasury. Together they worked to reduce regulations on businesses and to raise protective tariff rates. This made it easier for U.S. producers to sell goods at home. In response, Europeans also raised tariffs, making U.S. products more expensive there. Laws had been previously passed to break up monopolies and protect workers, but Harding favored less restriction on businesses. His Secretary of Commerce, **Herbert Hoover,** asked business leaders to voluntarily make advancements.

Harding admitted that he preferred playing golf or poker to governing. He trusted his friends with important government positions. One friend, Charles Forbes, wasted millions of dollars while running the Veterans' Bureau. Another, Secretary of the Interior Albert Fall, created the biggest scandal of Harding's administration. In the **Teapot Dome scandal,** Fall took bribes to transfer control of oil reserves from the United States Navy to private oilmen. Fall was later forced to return the oil and sentenced to a year in jail. Harding died in 1923, before the full extent of the scandal came to light.

The new President, **Calvin Coolidge,** was quiet and honest. He put his administration in the hands of men who held to the simple virtues of an older generation. Like Harding, he mistrusted the use of legislation to achieve social change. He favored big business. He reduced the national debt and lowered taxes to give incentives to businesses. However, Coolidge said and did nothing about the country's many problems, such as low prices for farm crops, racial discrimination, and low wages.

In foreign policy, Coolidge pushed European governments to repay war debts to the United States. In 1924, an agreement known as the **Dawes Plan** was arranged to help Germany, France, and Great Britain repay those debts. In 1928, exhausted by World War I, 62 nations signed the **Kellogg-Briand Pact,** a treaty that outlawed war. Unfortunately, there was no way for nations to enforce the treaty, and it was quickly forgotten.

Review Questions

1. What was the Teapot Dome scandal?

_____

_____

2. How did Presidents Harding and Coolidge feel about laws that restricted businesses?

_____

_____

Note Taking Study Guide
SOCIAL AND CULTURAL TENSIONS

Focus Question: How did Americans differ on major social and cultural issues?

As you read, look for issues that divided Americans in the 1920s.

Differing Viewpoints	
Education	• Viewpoint 1: • Viewpoint 2:
Evolution	• Viewpoint 1: • Viewpoint 2:
	• Viewpoint 1: • Viewpoint 2:
	• Viewpoint 1: • Viewpoint 2:
	• Viewpoint 1: • Viewpoint 2:

CHAPTER 11

SECTION 3

Section Summary

SOCIAL AND CULTURAL TENSIONS

What did the Eighteenth Amendment forbid?

_____

_____

_____

What does the word *imperial* mean in the underlined sentence? Look for context clues in the surrounding words and phrases. Circle any words or phrases in the paragraph that help you figure out what *imperial* means.

_____

_____

_____

Contrast Select an issue that divided Americans. Contrast the ways rural and urban Americans felt about this issue.

_____

_____

_____

As the 1920s began, striking differences arose between urban and rural America. Urban Americans enjoyed a rising standard of living and embraced a modern view of the world. City dwellers tended to value education and to be advocates of science and social change.

By contrast, in rural America times were hard. Formal education was considered less important than keeping the farm going. People tended to be conservative about political and social issues, preferring to keep things the way they were. Many rural Americans believed that the Bible was literally true. This belief was called **fundamentalism.** It opposed modernism, which stressed science.

The two beliefs clashed head-on in the 1925 **Scopes Trial.** That year, Tennessee passed a law making it illegal to teach the theory of evolution in the state's public schools. The most celebrated defense attorney in the country, **Clarence Darrow,** defended John Scopes for teaching this scientific theory to his high school class. Scopes was found guilty of breaking the law and fined $100.

A wave of immigration inspired nativist politicians to pass laws forcing immigrants to pass a literacy test, and to create a **quota system.** The quota system set limits on the number of new immigrants allowed into the United States. Although many Americans appreciated the nation's growing diversity, many did not. In 1915, the **Ku Klux Klan** was reorganized in Georgia. This violent group, whose leaders had titles such as Grand Dragon and Imperial Wizard, promoted hatred of African Americans, Jews, Catholics, and immigrants.

Another divisive issue of the 1920s was **Prohibition.** In 1919 the states ratified the **Eighteenth Amendment** to the Constitution, which forbade the manufacture, distribution, and sale (but not consumption) of alcohol. Congress then passed the **Volstead Act** to enforce the amendment. Police often turned a blind eye to illegal drinking establishments, which left room for **bootleggers** to not only sell alcohol but also to expand into other illegal activities, such as prostitution, drugs, robbery, and murder. Thus, Prohibition unintentionally led to the growth of organized crime.

Review Questions

1. What were some of the issues and beliefs that rural and urban America clashed over in the 1920s?

_____

_____

2. How did nativists feel about immigration?

_____

_____

CHAPTER 11 SECTION 4
Note Taking Study Guide
A NEW MASS CULTURE

Focus Question: How did the new mass culture reflect technological and social changes?

A. *As you read, look for examples of the ways in which American culture changed during the 1920s.*

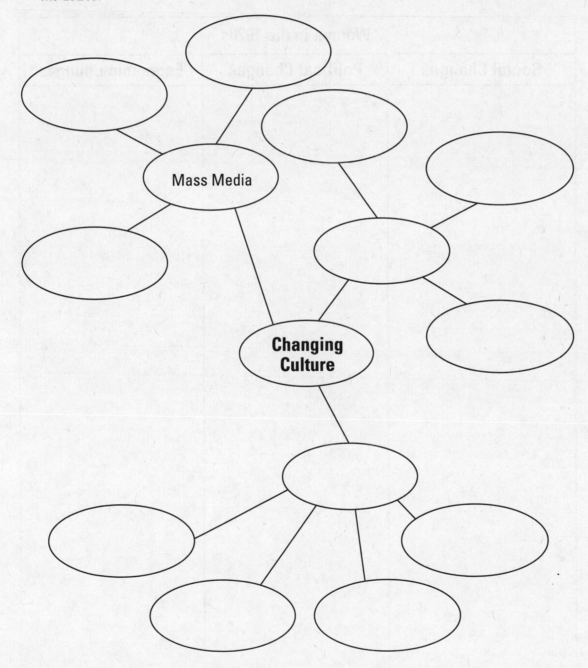

CHAPTER 11
SECTION 4

Note Taking Study Guide
A NEW MASS CULTURE

Focus Question: How did the new mass culture reflect technological and social changes?

B. *As you read, classify the various types of changes that took place in women's lives in the 1920s.*

Women in the 1920s		
Social Changes	**Political Changes**	**Economic Changes**
•	•	•
•	•	•
•		
•		

CHAPTER 11 SECTION 4

Section Summary
A NEW MASS CULTURE

As urban Americans' wages rose in the 1920s, workers also enjoyed shorter workweeks. For the first time, a large city-dwelling population had free time and money to spend on entertainment. One of the most popular forms of entertainment was movies, which were attended by 60 to 100 million Americans each week. Actors such as comedian **Charlie Chaplin,** heartthrob Rudolf Valentino, and cowboy William S. Hart became silent film stars. Then in 1927, the movie *The Jazz Singer* startled audiences when Al Jolson said, "You ain't seen nothin' yet." *The Jazz Singer* became the first movie to include sound matched to the action on the screen, and the era of "talkies" was born.

For entertainment at home, Americans bought millions of phonographs and radios. By 1923, almost 600 licensed radio stations broadcast to more than 600,000 radio sets. Americans across the continent listened to the same songs, learned the same dances, and shared a popular culture as never before. People admired the same heroes, such as baseball player **Babe Ruth,** the home-run king, and aviator **Charles Lindbergh,** who was the first to fly solo and non-stop across the Atlantic Ocean.

American women challenged political, economic, social, and educational boundaries. With passage of the Nineteenth Amendment, they won the right to vote. Many ran for political office and more joined the workforce. Some women, known as **flappers,** shocked society by wearing short skirts and bobbed hair. At home, new electric appliances made housework easier. Popular magazines, sociological studies, novels, and movies all featured the "New Woman" of the 1920s prominently.

A spirit of modernism grew, especially in cities. Austrian psychologist **Sigmund Freud** contributed to modernism with his theory that human behavior is driven by unconscious desires rather than by rational thought. Painters rejected artistic norms. Writers, including **F. Scott Fitzgerald** and **Ernest Hemingway,** wrote about the meaning of life and war. Their literary masterpieces examined subconscious desires and the dark side of the American dream.

Review Questions

1. What technological advances led to cultural change during the 1920s?

_____

_____

2. What changes in the 1920s allowed urban Americans to enjoy more entertainment?

_____

_____

READING CHECK

Who developed a theory about behavior and the unconscious?

_____

_____

_____

VOCABULARY STRATEGY

What does the word *sociological* mean in the underlined sentence? The term *socio* means "relating to society." The term *–ology* usually refers to a type of study. Use these definitions to help you figure out the meaning of *sociological.*

_____

_____

_____

READING SKILL

Summarize List three ways American culture changed in the 1920s.

_____

_____

_____

CHAPTER
11
SECTION 5

Note Taking Study Guide
THE HARLEM RENAISSANCE

Focus Question: How did African Americans express a new sense of hope and pride?

As you read, identify the main ideas.

I. New "Black Consciousness"

   A. New Chances, New Challenges

      1. Migration to North continues

      2. _____

      3. _____

   B. _____

      1. _____

      2. _____

      3. _____

II. _____

   A. _____

      1. _____

      2. _____

   B. _____

      1. _____

III. _____

   A. _____

      1. _____

   B. _____

      1. _____

CHAPTER 11 SECTION 5

Section Summary
THE HARLEM RENAISSANCE

Millions of African Americans left the South after World War I to find freedom and economic opportunity in the North. In the South, they faced low-paying jobs, substandard schools, Jim Crow oppression, and the threat of lynching. However, they found well-paying jobs, a middle class of African American professionals, and a growing political voice in cities such as New York, Chicago, and Detroit.

Harlem in New York City became a haven for about 200,000 African Americans from the South as well as black immigrants from the Caribbean. One immigrant was **Marcus Garvey,** a Jamaican who had traveled widely. After seeing that blacks were treated poorly, Garvey organized a "Back to Africa" movement that urged black unity and separation of the races.

It was F. Scott Fitzgerald who called the 1920s the "Jazz Age." However, it was African Americans who gave the age its **jazz.** A truly indigenous American musical form, jazz emerged in the South as a combination of African American and European musical styles. African Americans migrating north brought the new musical style with them. Musicians such as trumpet player **Louis Armstrong** took jazz to the world. Singer **Bessie Smith,** nicknamed the "Empress of the Blues," was so popular she became the highest-paid African American entertainer of the 1920s.

The decade also saw the **Harlem Renaissance,** an outpouring of art and literature that explored the African American experience. Among its most famous writers was **Claude McKay,** whose novels and poems were militant calls for action. **Langston Hughes** celebrated African American culture, and **Zora Neale Hurston** wrote about women's desire for independence.

The Great Depression ended the Harlem Renaissance. However, the pride and unity it created provided a foundation for the future civil rights movement.

Review Questions

1. Why did many African Americans migrate north?

_____

_____

2. What was the "Back to Africa" movement?

_____

_____

READING CHECK

What did F. Scott Fitzgerald name the 1920s?

_____

_____

_____

VOCABULARY STRATEGY

Find the word *indigenous* in the underlined sentence. What do you think it means? Circle words, phrases, or sentences in the surrounding paragraph to help you define *indigenous*.

_____

_____

_____

READING SKILL

Identify Main Ideas What was the Harlem Renaissance?

_____

_____

_____

Name _____ Class _____ Date _____

Focus Question: How did the prosperity of the 1920s give way to the Great Depression?

A. *Identify the causes of the Great Depression.*

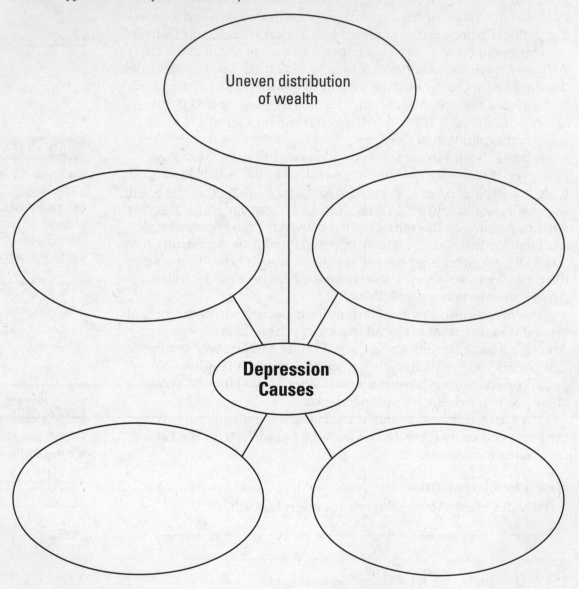

Uneven distribution of wealth

Depression Causes

Note Taking Study Guide
CAUSES OF THE DEPRESSION

Focus Question: How did the prosperity of the 1920s give way to the Great Depression?

B. *Use a flowchart to note what happened in the wake of the stock market crash.*

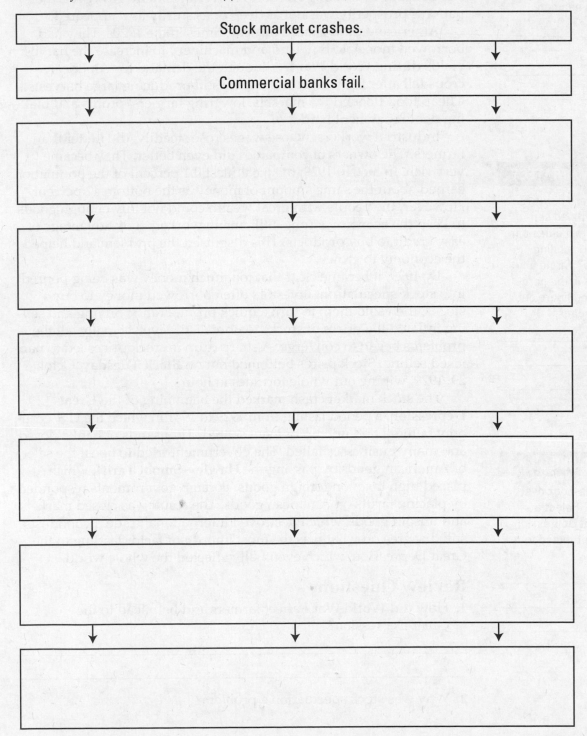

Stock market crashes.

Commercial banks fail.

CHAPTER 12 SECTION 1 — Section Summary

CAUSES OF THE DEPRESSION

The Roaring Twenties were a Republican decade. Beginning in 1920, Republican Presidents led the nation and took credit for the good economic times. In 1928, the country continued to support the Republicans by electing **Herbert Hoover** President. However, the nation's prosperity was not as deep or as sturdy as it appeared.

American farmers faced difficult times in the 1920s. They had borrowed money to buy land and machinery to increase the harvest yields during World War I. Although the demand for American crops fell after the war, farmers were still producing large harvests. Cheap food flooded the markets, lowering farmers' profits and making debt repayment hard.

Industrial workers, whose wages rose steadily, did better than farmers. The owners of companies did even better. They became very rich. In fact, in 1929, the wealthiest 0.1 percent of the population earned about the same amount of money as the bottom 42 percent. However, the people with great wealth could not buy enough goods to keep the economy strong. Still, many workers took advantage of easy credit to buy products. This disguised the problem and helped the economy to grow.

By 1929, it became clear that too much money was being poured into stock **speculation.** Investors often borrowed money to buy stocks, then sold them to turn a quick profit. Frantic buying and selling inflated the prices of stocks to unrealistic levels. <u>Finally, all the problems began to converge.</u> A sharp drop in stock prices led to panicked selling. Stock prices bottomed out on **Black Tuesday,** October 29, 1929, wiping out whole fortunes in hours.

The stock market crash marked the beginning of the **Great Depression,** a period lasting from 1929 to 1941 in which the U.S. economy faltered and unemployment soared. Thousands of banks closed and many businesses failed. The government tried to boost the sale of American goods by passing the **Hawley-Smoot Tariff,** which placed high taxes on foreign goods. Foreign governments responded by placing tariffs on American goods. The result was closed markets and unsold goods, which destroyed international trade. Economists still disagree on what was the most important factor leading to the Great Depression, which eventually affected the whole world.

Review Questions

1. How did World War I affect farmers and help lead to the Great Depression?

_____

_____

2. Why was stock speculation a problem?

_____

_____

Name _____ Class _____ Date _____

Focus Question: How did the Great Depression affect the lives of urban and rural Americans?

As you read, use the Venn diagram below to note how the depression affected both urban and rural America.

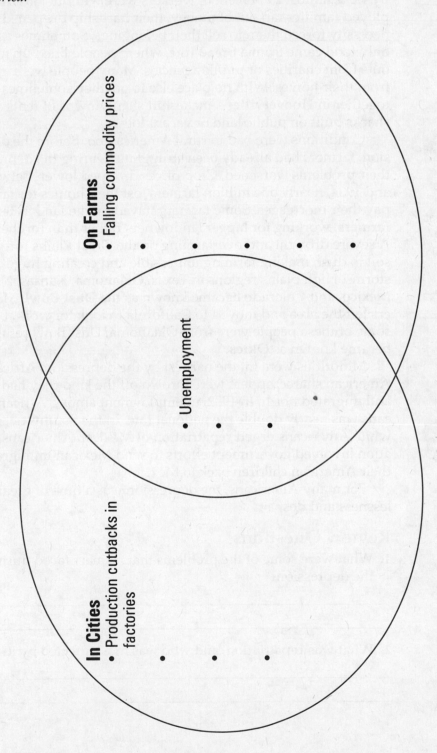

On Farms
- Falling commodity prices
- • • • • •

Unemployment
- • • •

In Cities
- Production cutbacks in factories
- • • •

Name _____ Class _____ Date _____

In what part of the country did the Dust Bowl occur?

_____

_____

_____

What does *drastic* mean in the underlined sentence? Read the underlined sentence aloud, but leave out the word *drastic*. What word could you use in its place? Use this strategy to help you figure out the meaning of *drastic*.

_____

_____

_____

Categorize Which of the following were present in both urban and rural America? Circle your answer.

• Hoovervilles

• Unemployment

• Farm foreclosures

The Great Depression deeply affected Americans. Some lost everything they had while others struggled simply to survive. In the cities, Americans faced rampant unemployment. Between 1921 and 1929, annual average unemployment rates never rose above 3.7 percent. By 1933, almost 25 percent of workers were without jobs. As unemployed families ran out of money, their hardship deepened. Drastic necessity forced them to sell their belongings. Sometimes a family's only food came from a **bread line**, where people lined up for handouts from charities or public agencies. Many people were evicted from their homes. With no place else to go, they sometimes grouped together in **Hoovervilles**—makeshift shantytowns of tents and shacks built on public land or vacant lots.

Conditions were bad in rural America, too. Before the depression, farmers had already been struggling. During the depression, their problems worsened. Crop prices dropped lower. Between 1930 and 1934, nearly one million farmers lost their homes for failure to pay their mortgages. Some farmers stayed on the land as **tenant farmers,** working for bigger landowners rather than for themselves. A severe drought and overfarming on the Great Plains turned the soil to dust, making farming impossible and creating huge dust storms. High plains regions in Texas, Oklahoma, Kansas, New Mexico, and Colorado became known as the **Dust Bowl.** Many farmers left the area and moved to California to look for work. Because some of these people were from Oklahoma, Dust Bowl refugees became known as **Okies.**

Minorities were hit the hardest by the depression. African American sharecroppers were thrown off the land they had farmed and migrated north. In 1932, unemployment among African Americans was nearly double the national rate. In the Southwest, many white Americans urged **repatriation** of Mexican Americans. Repatriation involved government efforts to send Mexican immigrants and their American children back to Mexico.

For many Americans, the depression was a time of great hopelessness and despair.

Review Questions

1. What were some of the problems that farmers faced during the depression?

_____

_____

2. What was repatriation, and who was most affected by it?

_____

_____

CHAPTER 12 SECTION 3

Note Taking Study Guide
HOOVER'S RESPONSE FAILS

Focus Question: Why did Herbert Hoover's policies fail to solve the country's economic crisis?

As you read, fill in the outline with details about President Hoover's response to the depression.

Hoover's Response to the Depression

I. Cautious Response Fails

   A. Hoover Tries Volunteerism

      1. Calls on business leaders to maintain employment, wages, prices

      2. _____

      3. _____

   B. Volunteerism Fails

      1. _____

      2. _____

II. More Activist Policies

   A. _____

      1. _____

      2. _____

   B. _____

      1. _____

      2. _____

      3. _____

      4. _____

   C. _____

      1. _____

      2. _____

      3. _____

CHAPTER 12 SECTION 3 — Section Summary
HOOVER'S RESPONSE FAILS

READING CHECK

Who led army troops against protesters in Washington, D.C., during the summer of 1932?

_____

_____

_____

VOCABULARY STRATEGY

What does the word *simultaneously* mean in the underlined sentence? Look for clues in the surrounding words, phrases, and sentences. Circle the phrase below that has the same meaning as *simultaneously*.

• done at the same time

• done one after the other

READING SKILL

Identify Supporting Details List the details that support the conclusion that Hoover's policy of volunteerism failed.

_____

_____

_____

From big cities to small towns, the Great Depression spread misery across America. As the crisis deepened, Herbert Hoover struggled to respond to the nation's problems.

At first, Hoover felt that government should not interfere with what he thought was the natural downswing of the business cycle. Soon, however, Hoover tried a different approach, called volunteerism. Hoover asked business leaders not to cut prices and wages. He called for the government to simultaneously reduce taxes, lower interest rates, and create public-works programs. He also asked the wealthy to give to the poor through charities. Finally, Hoover called for a policy of **localism.** This policy asked state and local governments to provide more jobs and relief measures. However, businesses cut wages and laid off workers, towns and states did not have the resources to respond to the crisis, and charities ran low on money. The crisis demanded federal action.

Next, the President decided to adopt a policy of **trickle-down economics.** The idea was that the government would provide loans to bankers so they in turn could lend money to businesses. Businesses would then hire workers, leading to increased production and consumption, and the end of the depression. At Hoover's urging, Congress created the **Reconstruction Finance Corporation (RFC)** to provide loans to businesses. However, businesses that did receive loans did not always use them to hire workers. Hoover did have one success in the building of **Hoover Dam.** Construction of the dam on the Colorado River brought much-needed employment to the Southwest in the early 1930s.

Americans became increasingly unhappy with Hoover's handling of the depression. A group of almost twenty thousand unemployed World War I veterans known as the **Bonus Army** marched in protest and set up camps in Washington, D.C. They wanted early payment of a bonus promised them. Congress agreed, but Hoover vetoed the plan. When riots broke out in July 1932, Hoover called in the military. General **Douglas MacArthur** led army troops against the veterans. Many of the veterans were hurt, a situation that angered many Americans. Hoover had little hope of reelection.

Review Questions

1. What was President Hoover's first response to the depression?

_____

_____

2. What was the Bonus Army?

_____

_____

CHAPTER
13
SECTION 1

Note Taking Study Guide

FDR OFFERS RELIEF AND RECOVERY

Focus Question: How did the New Deal attempt to address the problems of the depression?

Fill in the chart below with the problems that FDR faced and the steps he took to overcome them.

FDR Tackles Tough Problems	
Problem	**FDR's Policy**
Failing banks	•
	•
	• • •
	•
	• • • •

Name _____ Class _____ Date _____

<table>
<tr><td>CHAPTER
13
SECTION 1</td><td>**Section Summary**
FDR OFFERS RELIEF AND RECOVERY</td></tr>
</table>

READING CHECK

Name two New Deal policies that provided immediate relief to Americans.

_____

_____

_____

VOCABULARY STRATEGY

What does the word *subsidies* mean in the underlined sentence? What context clues can you find in the surrounding words or phrases? Circle any words or phrases in the paragraph that help you figure out what *subsidies* means.

_____

_____

_____

READING SKILL

Connect Ideas What parts of the U.S. economy were affected by FDR's New Deal policies?

_____

_____

_____

In November 1932, **Franklin D. Roosevelt** won the presidency by more than 7 million votes. FDR had lost the use of his legs to polio in 1921. Because of his disability, he relied heavily on his wife, **Eleanor Roosevelt.** She served as his "eyes and ears" during his presidency.

In his first hundred days in office, FDR proposed and Congress passed 15 bills known as the First **New Deal.** These measures had three goals: relief, recovery, and reform. "Relief" referred to improving the immediate hardships of the depression; "recovery" was aimed at achieving a long-term economic recovery; and "reforms" were designed to prevent future depressions. <u>One immediate relief effort involved the government paying farmers subsidies to reduce production, a move that would help raise farm prices.</u>

Other relief efforts included establishment of the **Tennessee Valley Authority (TVA)** to build dams in the Tennessee River valley to control floods and generate electric power, and the creation of the **Civilian Conservation Corps (CCC).** The CCC provided jobs for more than 2 million young men. They replanted forests, built trails, dug irrigation ditches, and fought fires. Recovery efforts included the **National Recovery Administration (NRA)** and the **Public Works Administration (PWA).** The NRA developed industry codes that set minimum wages for workers and minimum prices for goods. The PWA created millions of new jobs constructing bridges, dams, power plants, and government buildings. Additionally, FDR sought to reform the nation's financial institutions. The **Federal Deposit Insurance Corporation (FDIC)** insured bank deposits, and the Securities Exchange Commission (SEC) regulated the stock market.

Some Americans thought the New Deal made the government too powerful. Others thought that the New Deal did not provide enough help to citizens. The strongest criticism from this second group came from individuals with roots in the Populist movement. Father **Charles Coughlin** was a Roman Catholic priest who aired increasingly angry views on a weekly radio show. Roman Catholic officials eventually forced Coughlin to stop his broadcasts. Senator **Huey Long** of Louisiana proposed placing high taxes on wealthy Americans so that their income could be redistributed to the poor.

Review Questions

1. What were the three main goals of the New Deal?

_____

_____

2. How did critics respond to FDR's New Deal policies?

_____

_____

CHAPTER
13
SECTION 2

Note Taking Study Guide
THE SECOND NEW DEAL

Focus Question: What major issues did the second New Deal address?

Complete the table below to record problems and the second New Deal's solutions.

The Second New Deal	
Problem	**Solution**
Unemployment	

Name _____ Class _____ Date _____

President Franklin D. Roosevelt's goals for the first New Deal were relief, recovery, and reform. He used legislation passed by the **second New Deal** to accomplish the goals of promoting the general welfare and protecting citizens' rights.

In the spring of 1935, Congress created the **Works Progress Administration (WPA)** to provide new jobs doing public works. The WPA even provided programs to employ displaced artists. The government paid for WPA programs by spending money it didn't have. British economist **John Maynard Keynes** argued that such deficit spending was needed to end the depression.

The **Social Security Act** created a pension system for retirees, as well as unemployment insurance for workers who lost their jobs and aid for the disabled. New programs aided farmers. The Rural Electrification Administration (REA) helped bring electricity to farms. New laws also aided industrial workers. The **Wagner Act** gave workers the right to **collective bargaining.** This meant that employers had to negotiate with unions about hours, wages, and other working conditions. The **Fair Labor Standards Act** of 1938 established a minimum wage and a maximum number of hours for the workweek. It also outlawed child labor.

During the Great Depression, there was an upsurge in union activity. The **Congress of Industrial Organizations (CIO)** was established to organize workers in major industries. In 1936, CIO members staged a **sit-down strike** against General Motors, refusing to leave the workplace until a settlement had been reached. Their success led to other strikes, which improved wages and working conditions for union members.

FDR faced challenges from the Supreme Court, which struck down a number of the key laws of the New Deal. To dilute the power of the sitting Justices, FDR asked Congress to add six new Justices to the nine-member court, a plan that became known as **court packing.** After 1937, the Supreme Court became more willing to accept New Deal legislation. After a new economic downturn in 1938, FDR chose not to try to force more reforms through Congress.

Review Questions

1. Describe one New Deal program that promoted the general welfare.

_____

_____

2. Explain how New Deal legislation promoted the well-being of workers.

_____

_____

CHAPTER 13 SECTION 3

Note Taking Study Guide
EFFECTS OF THE NEW DEAL

Focus Question: How did the New Deal change the social, economic, and political landscape of the United States for future generations?

As you read, identify the lasting effects of the New Deal upon American society.

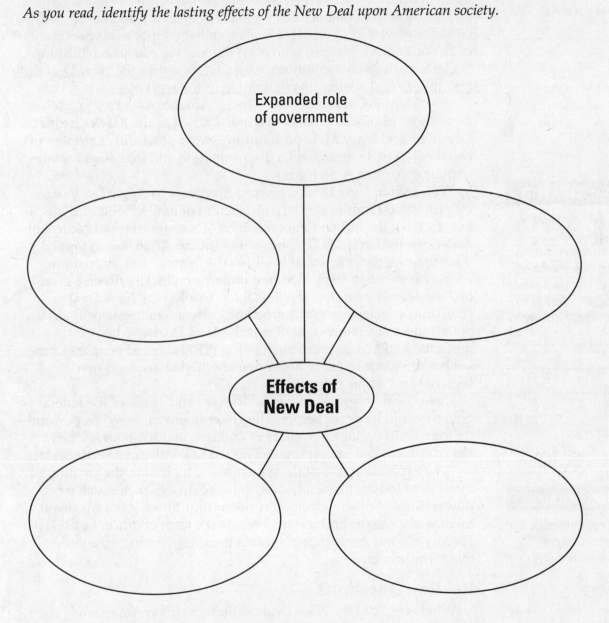

CHAPTER **13** SECTION 3	**Section Summary** EFFECTS OF THE NEW DEAL

How did the New Deal lead to the rise of a welfare state?

_____

_____

_____

What does the word *gender* mean in the underlined sentence? The paragraph it appears in discusses the role of women in the New Deal. Use the subject of the paragraph to help you figure out the meaning of *gender*.

_____

_____

_____

Identify Main Ideas How did the New Deal benefit different groups in American society?

_____

_____

_____

The New Deal brought fundamental changes to the nation. Some women were provided with the opportunity to increase their political influence. Eleanor Roosevelt transformed the office of First Lady to a politically active position. She traveled extensively and advocated equal justice for all. The first female Cabinet member was Secretary of Labor Frances Perkins, who played a leading role in establishing Social Security and a minimum wage. Despite this, the New Deal did not fight to end gender discrimination in the workplace.

President Roosevelt invited African American leaders to advise him. These unofficial advisers became known as the **Black Cabinet.** One member, **Mary McLeod Bethune,** was a powerful champion of racial equality. Even so, racial discrimination and injustice continued to plague African Americans.

The **Indian New Deal** was a program to help American Indians by providing funding for the construction of new schools and hospitals. In 1934, the Indian Reorganization Act restored tribal control of American Indian lands. The Bureau of Indian Affairs also stopped discouraging the practice of traditional American Indian customs.

By his death in 1945, FDR had united a culturally diverse group of Americans into a strong political force called the **New Deal coalition,** which gave the Democratic Party a sizable majority in both houses of Congress. FDR and the New Deal also helped to unify the nation. Programs such as the WPA allowed people of varied backgrounds to get to know one another, breaking down regional and ethnic prejudices.

New Deal programs increased the size and scope of the federal government like never before. The government assumed responsibility for providing for the welfare of children and the poor, elderly, sick, disabled, and unemployed. This led to the rise of a **welfare state.**

The expanding role of the government, including the creation of many new federal agencies, gave the executive branch much more power. Roosevelt was elected President four times. After his death, there was a call for limiting the President's term of office. In 1951, the Twenty-second Amendment limited the President to two consecutive terms in office.

Review Questions

1. What effect did the New Deal coalition have on American party politics?

_____

_____

2. How did Franklin D. Roosevelt expand the role of the federal government?

_____

_____

Name _____ Class _____ Date _____

Focus Question: How did the men and women of the depression find relief from their hardships in the popular culture?

As you read, complete the table below to record examples of cultural or popular media.

Cultural or Popular Media	Example
Movies	

Name _____ Class _____ Date _____

READING CHECK

What was the Federal Art Project?

_____

_____

_____

VOCABULARY STRATEGY

What does the word *episodes* mean in the underlined sentence? What clues can you find in the surrounding words, phrases, or sentences? Use these clues to help you determine the meaning of *episodes*.

_____

_____

_____

READING SKILL

Identify Main Ideas and Details In what ways were the 1930s a golden age for entertainment?

_____

_____

_____

Entertainment became big business during the 1930s, creating a golden age in American culture. Large radio networks dominated the airwaves, while a cluster of film companies ruled the silver screen. Radio ownership grew during the decade, and nearly two thirds of all Americans attended at least one movie a week.

The movies were a form of escapism during the Great Depression as Americans sought relief from their concerns. Movies like *The Wizard of Oz* promised weary audiences that their dreams really could come true. In the early 1930s, many films reflected the public's distrust of big business and government. Others, such as the films of **Frank Capra,** celebrated American idealism and the triumph of the common man over adversity.

Radio brought news and entertainment into American homes. FDR used fireside radio chats to explain his New Deal programs. National radio networks broadcast dramas, comedies, soap operas, and variety shows. Episodes from *The Lone Ranger* began running in 1933 and lasted for more than 20 years. Sometimes the lines between news and entertainment were blurred. When the Mercury Theatre broadcast a drama called *War of the Worlds* on October 30, 1938, many people panicked, believing that Martians were actually invading.

Music also provided a diversion from hard times, whether on the radio at home or in nightclubs. Americans enjoyed "swing" music played by "big bands." Blues singers focused on the harsh conditions faced by African Americans. Woody Guthrie wrote ballads about the Okies, farmers who fled the Dust Bowl.

The federal government funded the arts for the first time through programs such as the **Federal Art Project.** Artists painted huge **murals** on public buildings across the nation. **Dorothea Lange** and other photographers documented the plight of America's farmers.

Many writers produced novels featuring working-class heroes. **John Steinbeck's** *The Grapes of Wrath* traces the fictional Joad family from the Oklahoma Dust Bowl to California. **Lillian Hellman** wrote several plays featuring strong roles for women as well as screenplays for movies. Americans also enjoyed comic strips and comic books.

Review Questions

1. How did popular culture change during the 1930s?

_____

_____

2. What were some of the major themes of literature in the 1930s?

_____

_____

CHAPTER
14
SECTION 1

Note Taking Study Guide
DICTATORS AND WAR

Focus Question: Why did totalitarian states rise after World War I, and what did they do?

A. *As you read, summarize the actions in the 1930s of each of the countries listed in the table below.*

1930s Actions		
Japan	•	•
Germany	• • • •	
Italy	• • •	
Soviet Union	• •	

Name _____ Class _____ Date _____

Focus Question: Why did totalitarian states rise after World War I, and what did they do?

B. *Use the concept web below to record the main ideas about the policies of Great Britain, France, and the United States toward aggressive nations.*

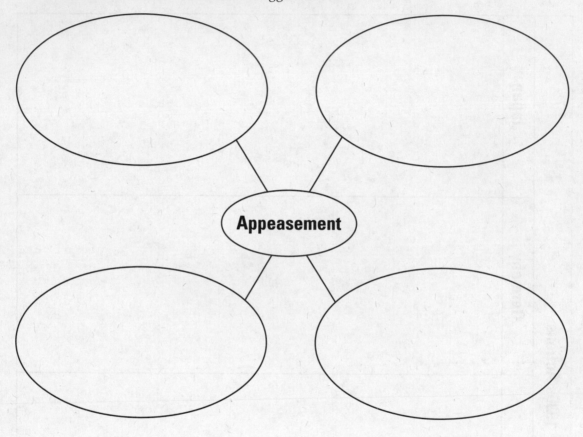

Appeasement

CHAPTER 14 SECTION 1

Section Summary

DICTATORS AND WAR

In the 1920s, some nations moved toward democracy. Others moved toward repressive dictatorships and **totalitarianism,** a type of government in which a single party or leader controls the economic, social, and cultural lives of its people.

The 1917 communist revolution in the Soviet Union produced the first totalitarian state, headed by Vladimir Lenin. In 1924, **Joseph Stalin** took his place as the Communist Party's head.

A postwar economic depression troubled Italy. In 1922, the king asked the founder of the Fascist Party, **Benito Mussolini,** to form a government. Mussolini turned Italy into a fascist country, with a controlled press, secret police, and no political parties.

Following World War I, Germany became a democracy. However, the Great Depression caused severe economic troubles in the 1930s. The National Socialist German Workers' Party (Nazi Party) led by **Adolf Hitler** rose to power. <u>Hitler criticized many people, political programs, and ideologies, but his sharpest assaults were against communists and Jews.</u> Hitler was violently **antisemitic,** or prejudiced against Jewish people. He was appointed chancellor in 1933 and became president of Germany within two years.

In Japan, the Great Depression ended a period of increased democracy and peaceful change. Military leaders argued that expansion throughout Asia would solve Japan's problems. Japan attacked Manchuria and established a puppet state in 1931. Six years later, Japan attacked China again, raiding the capital city with such brutality that it became known as the "Rape of Nanjing."

In the 1930s, Italy and Germany resorted to acts of aggression similar to those of Japan in Asia. Hitler reclaimed the Saar region from French control and sent troops into the Rhineland, while Mussolini led an invasion into Ethiopia. The League of Nations did almost nothing to stop the aggression.

France, Britain, and the United States pursued the policy of **appeasement** toward the fascist leaders. Appeasement means granting concessions to a potential enemy to maintain peace. However, this approach only encouraged the leaders to become bolder and more aggressive.

Review Questions

1. After World War I, what kind of government was set up in Germany? Who became the country's leader?

_____

_____

2. How did the military leaders of Japan want to solve the country's problems?

_____

_____

READING CHECK

How did Benito Mussolini come to rule Italy?

_____

_____

_____

VOCABULARY STRATEGY

What does the word *ideologies* mean in the underlined sentence? What context clues can you find in the surrounding words or phrases? Circle any words or phrases in the paragraph that help you figure out what *ideologies* means.

_____

_____

_____

READING SKILL

Summarize Name the countries and leaders discussed in this section.

_____

_____

_____

Name _____ Class _____ Date _____

Focus Question: How did Americans react to events in Europe and Asia in the early years of World War II?

Sequence the major events described in the section using the timeline below.

Atlantic Charter issued — **Aug. 1941**

Germany invades Poland. — **Sept. 1939**

Section Summary
FROM ISOLATION TO INVOLVEMENT

After Japan's violent attack on China in 1937, President Roosevelt criticized the Japanese aggression. The United States, however, continued to back away from intervention in foreign conflicts.

Despite a military alliance among France, Britain, and Poland, Germany invaded Poland in 1939. Britain and France declared war on Germany, and World War II had begun. The **Axis Powers** would come to include Germany, Italy, Japan, and several other nations. The Axis Powers fought the **Allies,** which included Britain, France, and eventually the Soviet Union, China, and the United States.

Germany used a new technique called **blitzkrieg,** or "lightning war." Tanks and planes attacked in a coordinated effort and quickly conquered Poland. In April 1940, Denmark and Norway fell to the German blitzkrieg. In May, Germany took the Netherlands, Belgium and Luxembourg, and then invaded France. The next month, Germany attacked Britain from the air.

Winston Churchill, the prime minister of Britain, hoped to convince America to join the Allies. Reports by news reporter Edward R. Murrow on the bombing of London shocked the American public. Murrow emphasized that the Germans were bombing civilians, not armies or military sites. Despite its isolationist policies, the United States moved slowly toward involvement. Congress passed the **Neutrality Act of 1939.** This law helped the Allies buy goods and munitions from the United States. Isolationists, however, believed that getting involved in a bloody European war would be wasteful and dangerous.

Even though most Americans wanted to remain neutral, President Roosevelt constantly argued for helping Britain. In early 1941, Congress approved the **Lend-Lease Act.** This act gave the President the power to sell, give, or lease weapons to protect the United States. In 1941, Roosevelt also met with Churchill to discuss the war. They signed the **Atlantic Charter,** a document that endorsed national self-determination and an international system of "general security." The agreement signaled the deepening alliance between the two nations. Hitler was not blind to American support of the Allies. In the fall of 1941, he ordered German U-boats to attack American ships. U.S. involvement in the war seemed inevitable.

Review Questions
1. What nations made up the Axis Powers?

_____

_____

2. What was President Roosevelt's position on the war in Europe?

_____

_____

READING CHECK

What is a blitzkrieg?

_____

_____

_____

VOCABULARY STRATEGY

What does the word *coordinated* mean in the underlined sentence? What clues can you find in the surrounding words, phrases, or sentences? Circle the words in the underlined passage that could help you learn what *coordinated* means.

_____

_____

_____

READING SKILL

Sequence List the countries Germany conquered by order of date.

_____

_____

_____

Name _____ Class _____ Date _____

Focus Question: How did the United States react to the Japanese attack on Pearl Harbor?

A. *As you read, record the causes and effects of the attack on Pearl Harbor, as well as details about the attack itself, in the chart below.*

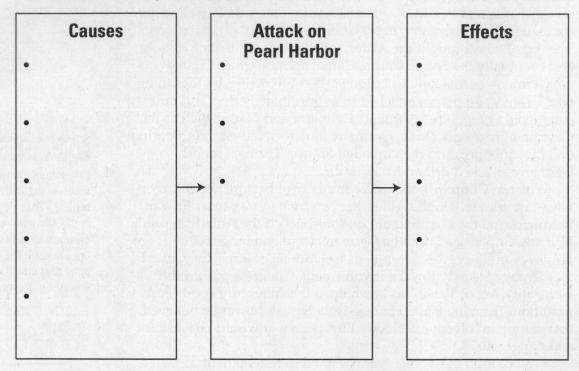

Causes	Attack on Pearl Harbor	Effects
•	•	•
•	•	•
•	•	•
•		•
•		

B. *Sequence the fighting that followed Pearl Harbor in the timetable below.*

Early War in the Pacific	
May 1942	The Philippines fall to the Japanese.

CHAPTER 14 SECTION 3

Section Summary

AMERICA ENTERS THE WAR

As Japan expanded its empire throughout Asia, its relationship with the United States worsened. Japan needed resources such as oil, steel, and rubber to maintain its military. The United States began to withhold these goods to limit Japan's expansion. The United States also instituted a trade embargo against Japan.

At first, **Hideki Tojo,** the Japanese prime minister, tried to keep the United States neutral. However, when a trade agreement with the United States failed, Tojo decided on a decisive military strike. On December 7, 1941, hundreds of Japanese airplanes bombed the site of the United States Navy's main base in the Pacific at **Pearl Harbor,** Hawaii. Nearly 2,500 people were killed in this devastating surprise attack. Many ships were sunk, and hundreds of aircraft were destroyed or damaged.

Congress immediately declared war on Japan. Germany and Italy then declared war on the United States. Men joined the military by the millions. Thousands of women joined the **Women's Army Corps (WAC)** as clerical workers, truck drivers, instructors, and lab technicians. The government also created agencies to ensure the production of military equipment. <u>These agencies allocated scarce materials to the proper industries.</u>

In Asia, United States Army General **Douglas MacArthur** struggled unsuccessfully to hold the Philippines against the Japanese forces. U.S. forces finally had to retreat, and MacArthur evacuated to Australia. Some 75,000 U.S. troops fell back to the Bataan Peninsula and Corregidor Island where, in May 1942, they had to surrender. Japanese troops forced these sick and malnourished men to march many miles. More than 7,000 American and Filipino troops died on the march, which is known as the **Bataan Death March.**

By the summer of 1942, Japan controlled Southeast Asia and the western Pacific. Then in May 1942, the United States Navy finally began to stop the Japanese advance. At the **Battle of Coral Sea,** the United States Navy prevented Japan from taking a key spot in New Guinea. The impressive Japanese offensive was over.

Review Questions

1. Why did the United States begin a trade embargo against Japan?

_____

_____

2. What happened to U.S. forces in the Philippines?

_____

_____

READING CHECK

Why was the Battle of Coral Sea so important to the United States?

_____

_____

_____

VOCABULARY STRATEGY

What does the word *allocated* mean in the underlined sentence? What clues can you find in the surrounding words, phrases, or sentences? Circle the words in the underlined passage that could help you learn what *allocated* means.

_____

_____

_____

READING SKILL

Identify Causes and Effects
What was the United States' immediate reaction to the attack on Pearl Harbor?

_____

_____

_____

CHAPTER 15 SECTION 1

Note Taking Study Guide

THE ALLIES TURN THE TIDE

Focus Question: How did the Allies turn the tide against the Axis?

List the ways in which the Allies turned back the Axis advance.

Turning Back the Axis	
In Europe	**In the Pacific**
• Battle against U-boats in Atlantic	•
•	
	•
•	
	•
•	
•	
•	

CHAPTER 15 SECTION 1

Section Summary
THE ALLIES TURN THE TIDE

The attack on Pearl Harbor brought the United States into World War II. <u>The Allies' ultimate goal was to fight and win a two-front war.</u> Their first objective, however, was to defeat Hitler. The United States was producing millions of tons of guns, tanks, and other war supplies. German U-boats, however, had sunk over 3,500 merchant ships bound for Britain. By mid-1943, using radar, bombers, and underwater depth charges, Allied forces were sinking U-boats faster than Germany could manufacture them. The Allies had begun to win the war in the North Atlantic.

In 1941, Germany attacked Russia, and Stalin wanted Roosevelt and Churchill to open a second front in France. Instead, in early 1942, British planes began **saturation bombing,** dropping large numbers of bombs on German cities. American bombers used **strategic bombing,** targeting key political and industrial centers. The **Tuskegee Airmen,** an African American fighter squadron, played a key role in the bombing campaign. In January 1943, after the long, bitter Battle of Stalingrad, the Russians turned back the German invasion of their country. During the same month, FDR announced that only the **unconditional surrender** of the Axis Powers would end the war. That is, they had to give up completely.

To help pave the way for an invasion of Italy, the Allies decided to push the Germans out of North Africa, where they had been fighting British troops since 1940. In February 1942, American General **Dwight Eisenhower** commanded the Allied invasion. After difficult battles, General **George S. Patton, Jr.** took charge of American forces. In May 1943, German and Italian forces in North Africa surrendered. Two months later, Allied forces invaded Sicily, two miles off the mainland of Italy. From there, they launched their invasion of Italy, and in September, Italy surrendered.

In spite of its "Europe first" strategy, the United States did not ignore the Pacific where Japanese forces had continued to advance. In June 1942, the Japanese attacked Midway, a vital American naval base in the central Pacific. The American naval commander, Admiral **Chester Nimitz,** had learned of the Japanese plans, and the **Battle of Midway** was a decisive American victory. It ended Japanese expansion in the Pacific and put Japan on the defensive.

Review Questions
1. What tactics did the Allies use to weaken Germany?

_____

_____

2. Why was it so important for the United States to defeat the Japanese at Midway?

_____

_____

READING CHECK

Who were the Tuskegee Airmen?

_____

_____

_____

VOCABULARY STRATEGY

What does the word *ultimate* mean in the underlined sentence? Circle the word below that is a synonym for *ultimate.*

• first

• final

READING SKILL

Summarize How did the Allies prepare for the invasion of Italy?

_____

_____

_____

Name _____ Class _____ Date _____

Note Taking Study Guide

THE HOME FRONT

Focus Question: How did the war change America at home?

As you read, identify the major effects of World War II on the home front.

The Home Front, World War II		
Economy	**Effects on Women**	**Effects on Minorities**
• War bonds • Wage controls • • •	• • • • •	• • • • •

CHAPTER 15 SECTION 2

Section Summary

THE HOME FRONT

World War II fears and tensions tested civil liberties, but the war also provided new opportunities for women and minorities. Many women found jobs, especially in heavy industry. They gained confidence, knowledge, organizational experience, and a paycheck. However, few African Americans found meaningful employment with defense employers. In response, African American labor leader **A. Philip Randolph** planned a massive march on Washington, D.C., to protest employment discrimination. Under pressure, FDR issued **Executive Order 8802.** It assured fair hiring practices in any job funded with government money.

Wartime needs encouraged people to move to the South and Southwest to find jobs in defense industries. To alleviate the rural population drain, the United States initiated the **bracero program.** This program brought Mexican laborers to work on American farms. Although they often faced discrimination, braceros contributed greatly to the war effort.

After the attack on Pearl Harbor, the federal government moved 100,000 Japanese Americans living on the West Coast to camps in isolated locations under a policy of **internment.** There, they were held in jail-like conditions for the duration of the war. Some Japanese Americans went to court to seek their rights. In the 1944 case of *Korematsu* **v.** *United States,* the Supreme Court upheld the government's wartime internment policy. When the government lifted a ban on Japanese Americans serving in the armed forces, many enlisted. The Japanese American **442nd Regimental Combat Team** fought in the Italian campaign and became the most decorated military unit in American history.

The war cost Americans $330 billion. To help pay for it, Congress levied a tax on all working Americans. To ensure that there would be adequate raw materials, such as oil and rubber, for war production, **rationing** was instituted. The federal **Office of War Information (OWI)** worked with the media to encourage support of the war effort. Millions of Americans bought war bonds and contributed to the war effort in many other ways, large and small.

Review Questions

1. How did World War II change women's lives?

_____

_____

2. How did World War II affect Japanese Americans?

_____

_____

READING CHECK

What was the bracero program?

_____

_____

_____

VOCABULARY STRATEGY

What does the word *initiated* mean in the underlined sentence? Read the underlined sentence and the sentence that follows aloud, but leave out the word *initiated.* Think about what word could be used in its place. Use this strategy to help you figure out the meaning of *initiated.*

_____

_____

_____

READING SKILL

Identify Main Ideas How did the workplace change as a result of World War II?

_____

_____

_____

CHAPTER 15
SECTION 3

Note Taking Study Guide

VICTORY IN EUROPE AND THE PACIFIC

Focus Question: How did the Allies defeat the Axis Powers?

Identify the steps that led to the Allied victory.

Europe	**The Pacific**
• Allies land at Normandy on D-Day.	•
•	
	•
•	
	•
•	
	•
•	
	•

Allies Win World War II

CHAPTER 15 SECTION 3

Section Summary

VICTORY IN EUROPE AND THE PACIFIC

In 1943, the Allied leaders agreed to open a second front in France. On June 6, 1944, known as **D-Day,** British and American forces invaded France from the west, across the English Channel. More than 11,000 planes prepared the way, followed by more than 4,400 ships and landing crafts. By the end of the day, they had gained a toehold in France. By July 1, more than one million Allied troops had landed.

Germany now faced a hopeless two-front war, as the Soviets advanced from the east. In December 1944, Hitler ordered a counterattack, known as the **Battle of the Bulge.** <u>Hitler's scenario called for German forces to capture communication and transportation hubs.</u> The attack almost succeeded. However, with help from their bombers, the Allies managed to push the Germans out of France. By January 1945, the Soviet Army had reached the Oder River outside Berlin, and in April, the United States Army was just 50 miles west of Berlin. Hitler committed suicide on April 30, and on May 7, Germany surrendered.

American forces in the Pacific followed an **island-hopping** strategy in a steady path toward Japan. Japanese troops fought hard, and Japanese **kamikaze** pilots deliberately crashed their planes into American ships. By April 1945, American pilots finally made their way to Okinawa, 340 miles from Japan. From Okinawa, American pilots could bomb the Japanese home islands. American bombers hit factories, military bases, and cities.

Advances in technology helped determine the final outcome of the war. **Albert Einstein,** a famous scientist, had alerted FDR to the need to proceed with atomic development. Physicist **J. Robert Oppenheimer** was in charge of the scientific aspect of the program, known as the **Manhattan Project.** On the morning of July 16, 1945, the first atomic bomb was tested. In order to save American lives and to end the war, President **Harry S. Truman** decided to use the atomic bomb against Japan. On August 6, 1945, U.S. pilots dropped an atomic bomb on Hiroshima. Three days later, the United States dropped a second atomic bomb on Nagasaki. Emperor Hirohito made the decision to surrender, and on August 15, the Allies celebrated V-J (Victory in Japan) Day. World War II had been the most costly war in history. As many as 60 million people—mostly civilians—had died in the conflict.

Review Questions

1. What was involved in the D-Day invasion of France?

_____

_____

2. How did the Allies bring about the surrender of Japan?

_____

_____

READING CHECK

What was the Manhattan Project?

_____

_____

_____

VOCABULARY STRATEGY

What does the word *scenario* mean in the underlined sentence? Circle any words or phrases in the paragraph that help you figure out what *scenario* means.

_____

_____

_____

READING SKILL

Recognize Sequence Number the following events in chronological order.

_____ Japan surrenders.

_____ The first atomic bomb is tested.

_____ Germany surrenders.

Name _____ Class _____ Date _____

Focus Question: How did the Holocaust develop and what were its results?

A. *As you read, identify the steps that led to Hitler's attempt to exterminate European Jews.*

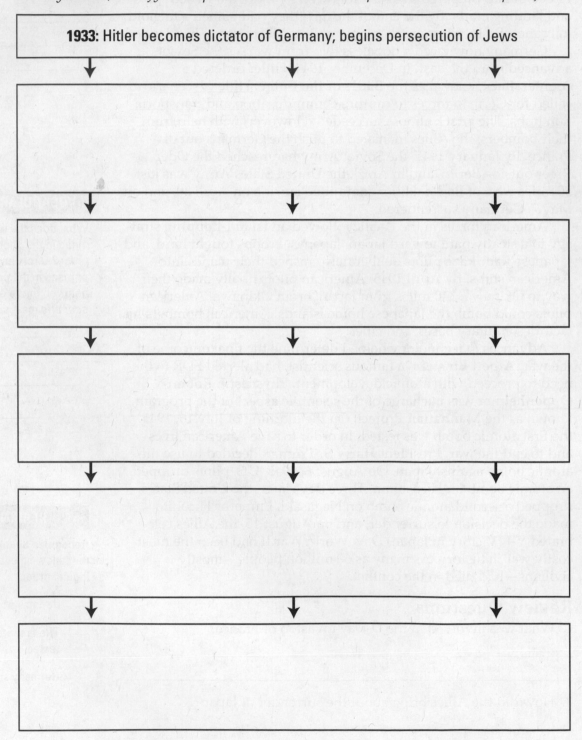

1933: Hitler becomes dictator of Germany; begins persecution of Jews

CHAPTER
15
SECTION 4

Note Taking Study Guide
THE HOLOCAUST

Focus Question: How did the Holocaust develop and what were its results?

B. *As you read, identify different ways in which the United States and other nations responded to the treatment of Jews in Nazi Germany before, during, and after the war.*

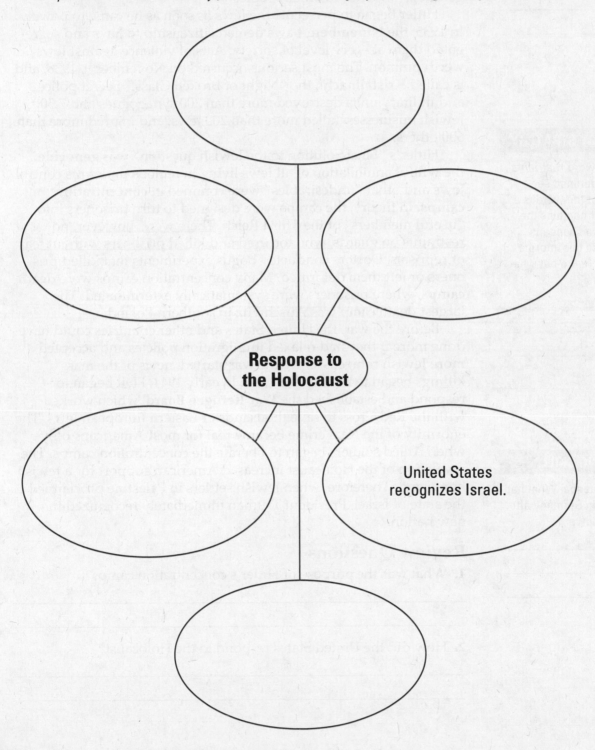

Response to the Holocaust

United States recognizes Israel.

Name _____ Class _____ Date _____

READING CHECK

What was Kristallnacht?

_____

_____

_____

In 1945, there was no word for the **Holocaust,** the most horrific event of World War II. It was the Nazi attempt to kill all Jews, as well as other "undesirables," under their control. This was part of a racist Nazi ideology that considered Aryans—white Northern European gentiles—superior to other people.

Hitler began to persecute the Jews as soon as he came to power. In 1935, the **Nuremberg Laws** denied citizenship to Jews and segregated them at every level of society. Acts of violence against Jews were common. The most serious occurred on November 9, 1938, and is called **Kristallnacht,** the "Night of Broken Glass." Secret police and military units destroyed more than 200 synagogues and 7,500 Jewish businesses, killed more than 200 Jews, and injured more than 600 others.

Hitler's "Final Solution to the Jewish question" was **genocide,** the willful annihilation of all Jews living in regions under his control. Jews and other "undesirables" were confined in **concentration camps.** In theory, the camps were designed to turn prisoners into "useful members" of the Third Reich. There were, however, no restraints on guards, who tortured and killed prisoners without fear of reprisals. Doctors conducted bogus experiments that killed prisoners or left them deformed. Many concentration camps were **death camps,** where prisoners were systematically exterminated. The largest death camp was Auschwitz in southern Poland.

Before the war, the United States and other countries could have done more if they had relaxed immigration policies and accepted more Jewish refugees. Once the war started, news of the mass killings began to filter to the West. In early 1944, FDR began to respond and established the **War Refugee Board,** which worked with the Red Cross to save thousands of Eastern European Jews. The enormity of the Nazi crime became real for most Americans only when Allied soldiers began to liberate the concentration camps. The revelation of the Holocaust increased American support for a Jewish homeland. Therefore, when Jewish settlers in Palestine proclaimed the state of Israel, President Truman immediately recognized the new nation.

VOCABULARY STRATEGY

What does the word *restraints* mean in the underlined sentence? Note that the word is a noun, and that it contains the verb *restrain,* which means "hold back." Use this information to help you figure out what *restraints* means.

_____

_____

_____

READING SKILL

Recognize Sequence What happened to Jews in Germany after Hitler came to power?

_____

_____

_____

Review Questions

1. What was the purpose of Hitler's concentration camps?

_____

_____

2. How did the United States respond to the Holocaust?

_____

_____

Name _____ Class _____ Date _____

Focus Question: What were the major immediate and long-term effects of World War II?

As you read, look for various developments in the postwar world that resulted from World War II.

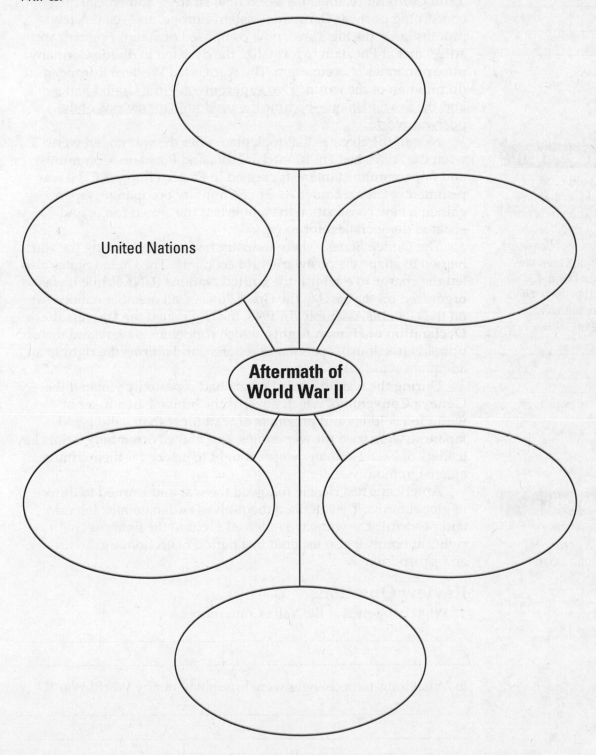

United Nations

Aftermath of World War II

CHAPTER 15 SECTION 5

Section Summary
EFFECTS OF THE WAR

READING CHECK

What is the Universal Declaration of Human Rights?

_____

_____

_____

VOCABULARY STRATEGY

What does the word *predominant* mean in the underlined sentence? The prefix *pre-* means "before in rank" or "superior to." The root *dominant* refers to something that dominates, controls, or has the greatest effect. Use these clues to help you figure out what *predominant* means.

_____

_____

_____

READING SKILL

Understand Effects Which effect of World War II would help to prevent future wars?

_____

_____

_____

As World War II drew to an end, Japan and Germany kept fighting long after their defeat was certain. The protracted fighting gave the Allies time to make plans for a postwar world. In February 1945, Roosevelt, Churchill, and Stalin met at Yalta on the Black Sea. At the **Yalta Conference,** they discussed final strategy and crucial questions concerning postwar Germany, Eastern Europe, and Asia. A few months later, the Big Three, now composed of Stalin, Truman, and Atlee, met at Potsdam to formalize the decision to divide Germany into four zones of occupation. The war ended Western European domination of the world. Two **superpowers**—the United States and the Soviet Union—became the predominant nations of the postwar world.

Not all the changes that took place after the war ended were what the Allies had envisioned at Yalta and Potsdam. Communist and noncommunist interests clashed in Eastern Europe. Civil war resumed in China. Under American military occupation, Japan gained a new constitution that abolished the armed forces and enacted democratic reforms.

The United States, where industry had boomed during the war, helped to shape the postwar world economy. The United States also led the charge to establish the **United Nations (UN).** While it was organized on the basis of the Great Powers, all member nations sat on the General Assembly. In 1948, the UN issued the **Universal Declaration of Human Rights,** which condemns slavery and torture, upholds freedom of speech and religion, and affirms the right to an adequate standard of living.

During the war, the Axis Powers had repeatedly violated the **Geneva Convention,** which governs the humane treatment of wounded soldiers and prisoners of war. More than a thousand Japanese were tried for war crimes, and at the **Nuremberg Trials** key leaders of Nazi Germany were brought to justice for their crimes against humanity.

Americans had closely followed the war and learned to think in global terms. They defined themselves as democratic, tolerant, and peaceful. The war gave renewed vigor to the fight for civil rights at home. It also ushered in a period of economic growth and prosperity.

Review Questions

1. What happened at the Yalta Conference?

_____

_____

2. What long-term changes were brought about by World War II?

_____

_____

CHAPTER 16 SECTION 1
Note Taking Study Guide
THE COLD WAR BEGINS

Focus Question: How did U.S. leaders respond to the threat of Soviet expansion in Europe?

A. *As you read, contrast the conflicting goals of the United States and the Soviet Union.*

American Goals	Soviet Goals

Name _____ Class _____ Date _____

Focus Question: How did U.S. leaders respond to the threat of Soviet expansion in Europe?

B. *As you read, trace events and developments in Europe that contributed to the growth of Cold War tensions.*

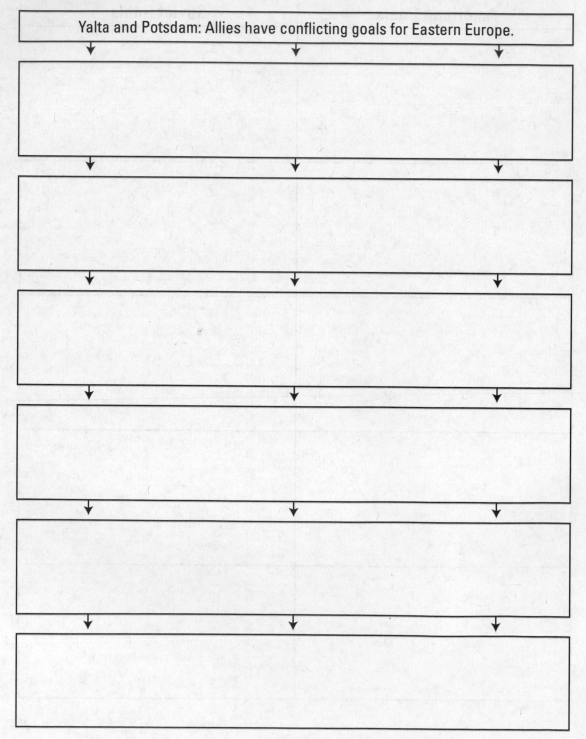

Yalta and Potsdam: Allies have conflicting goals for Eastern Europe.

CHAPTER 16 SECTION 1

Section Summary
THE COLD WAR BEGINS

When Roosevelt, Stalin, and Churchill met at Yalta in February 1945, it was clear that the Allies would defeat Germany. The United States and Great Britain wanted a united Germany and independent nations in Eastern Europe after the war. Soviet dictator Stalin wanted a weak, divided Germany and an Eastern Europe under communist control. Despite Stalin's promises, Poland, Czechoslovakia, Hungary, Romania, and Bulgaria became **satellite states** of the Soviet Union, along with the eastern part of Germany. <u>After another meeting that summer at Potsdam, Harry S. Truman, who was now President, became convinced that the Soviet Union had aspirations toward world domination.</u> Thus began the 46-year-long **Cold War.**

Churchill agreed with President Truman and said an **iron curtain** had descended upon Europe. East of the curtain, Stalin was tightening his grip and trying to spread communism to other countries. Truman asked Congress for money to help Turkey and Greece fight communism. His promise of aid became known as the **Truman Doctrine.** It set a new course for American foreign policy.

The goal of another American policy, called **containment,** was to use American power to help nations resist communism. Containment's first success was based on Secretary of State George C. Marshall's economic recovery plan for Europe. Under the **Marshall Plan,** the United States gave about $13 billion in grants and loans to Western European nations, starting in 1948.

In June 1948, Stalin decided to block all shipping from western Germany into West Berlin—deep inside communist East Germany— hoping that would make the city fall to the communists. The United States and Britain stopped his plan by airlifting supplies, including food, fuel, and clothing, into West Berlin.

The **Berlin airlift** showed that communism could be contained. To continue to block Soviet expansion, the **North Atlantic Treaty Organization, NATO,** formed in 1949. Twelve Western European and North American nations agreed to act together to defend Western Europe. In 1955, West Germany joined NATO. In response, the Soviet Union and its satellite states formed the **Warsaw Pact.** All communist states of Eastern Europe except Yugoslavia promised to defend one another if attacked.

Review Questions

1. What was Truman's promise of aid to countries fighting communism called?

_____

_____

2. Which event proved that the policy of containment worked?

_____

_____

READING CHECK

President Truman asked Congress for aid for which two countries?

_____

_____

_____

VOCABULARY STRATEGY

What does the word *aspirations* mean in the underlined sentence? Circle the words in the underlined sentence that could help you learn what *aspirations* means.

_____

_____

_____

READING SKILL

Contrast After World War II, what were the differences in goals between Stalin and the Soviets and Truman and the United States?

_____

_____

_____

CHAPTER 16 SECTION 2

Note Taking Study Guide

THE KOREAN WAR

Focus Question: How did President Truman use the power of the presidency to limit the spread of communism in East Asia?

As you read, note problems and the steps that President Truman took to solve them. Use the problem-solution table below.

Problem	Solution
Communists threaten takeover of China.	

Name _____ Class _____ Date _____

Since the Russian Revolution, the Soviets had tried to export communism around the world, sure that it would reach worldwide influence. Events in China in 1949 seemed to prove them right.

Chinese Nationalist leader **Jiang Jieshi** (known as Chiang Kai-shek in the United States) and communist leader **Mao Zedong** had been allies against Japan during World War II, but once the war ended, they became enemies. The United States supported Jiang, while the Soviet Union aided Mao. In 1949, Mao's communists took over the Chinese mainland, calling their government the People's Republic of China.

From there, the conflict over communism moved to Korea. After World War II, the United States and the Soviet Union had split Korea into two nations divided by the **38th parallel** of latitude. On June 25, 1950, about 90,000 North Korean troops armed with Soviet weapons crossed the 38th parallel to attack South Korea.

President Truman sent American troops to join South Korean and United Nations forces. Under the World War II hero General **Douglas MacArthur,** they attacked the port city of Inchon in September 1950. By October, they drove the North Koreans back north.

Truman worried what China might do if the war continued, but MacArthur told him China would not intervene and he continued to push northward. Then, on November 26, 1950, around 300,000 Chinese soldiers attacked. Truman did not want the United States to enter into a major war that would involve huge numbers of troops and maybe even atomic weapons, but MacArthur distrusted Truman's policy of a **"limited war."** When MacArthur sent a letter to Congress condemning the policy, Truman fired him.

By the spring of 1951, the war settled into a stalemate. To achieve a cease-fire in 1953, Dwight D. Eisenhower, now President, hinted he might use nuclear weapons.

No side won the Korean War, and the two Koreas remain divided today. But two things did change: Truman's use of American forces enlarged the power of the presidency, and a new alliance called the **Southeast Asia Treaty Organization (SEATO)** was formed to prevent the spread of communism. It was the Asian version of NATO.

Review Questions

1. What is the significance of the 38th parallel?

_____

_____

2. What was President Eisenhower's role in the cease-fire that ended the Korean War?

_____

_____

READING CHECK

What did China do that MacArthur insisted would not happen?

_____

_____

_____

VOCABULARY STRATEGY

What does the word *intervene* mean in the underlined sentence? Look at the context clues in the sentence to help you figure out what the word means. Circle the words that could help you learn what *intervene* means.

_____

_____

_____

READING SKILL

Categorize What idea and event led directly to Truman's firing of MacArthur?

_____

_____

_____

CHAPTER
16
SECTION 3

Note Taking Study Guide
THE COLD WAR EXPANDS

Focus Question: What methods did the United States use in its global struggle against the Soviet Union?

Identify the tactics used to wage the Cold War.

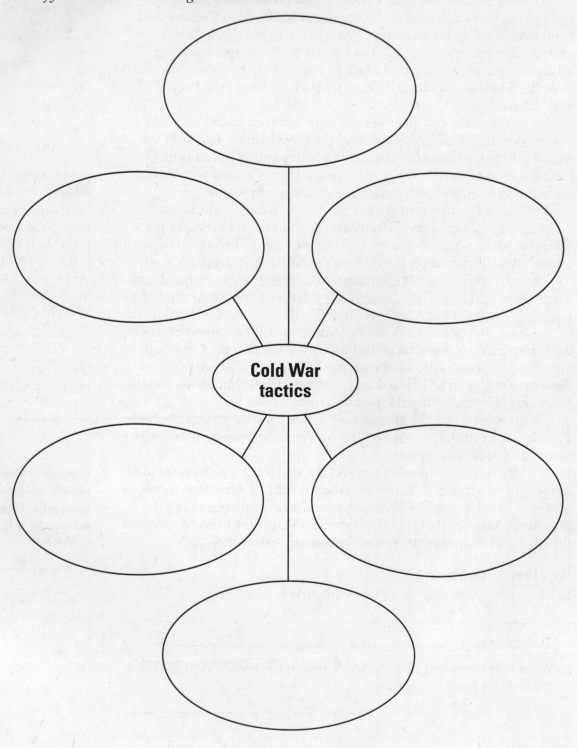

Cold War
tactics

CHAPTER 16 — SECTION 3

Section Summary

THE COLD WAR EXPANDS

On September 2, 1949, America learned that the Soviets now had an atomic bomb. The following month, communists took over China. For Americans, the world had suddenly become more threatening.

Truman soon ordered the development of a hydrogen bomb. Some scientists warned that developing the H-Bomb would lead to a perpetual **arms race.** For the next four decades, the United States and the Soviet Union stockpiled nuclear weapons. Each hoped this program of **mutually assured destruction** would prevent the other from actually using the weapons.

President Dwight D. Eisenhower continued to stockpile nuclear weapons. His foreign policy emphasized **massive retaliation.** Eisenhower's Secretary of State, **John Foster Dulles,** believed that only by going to the brink of war—an approach called **brinkmanship** —could the United States discourage communist aggression.

Nikita Khrushchev, who became leader of the Soviet Union in 1953, continued to try to spread communism. In 1956, workers in Poland rioted against Soviet rule and won greater control of their government. But when students and workers in Hungary tried the same thing, Khrushchev crushed the revolt.

In the Middle East, Egypt's president, Gamal Abdel Nasser, wanted to build a dam on the Nile River. When he opened relations with communist China and the Soviet Union, the United States withdrew its offer to help. Nasser then **nationalized** the Suez Canal. In response, Britain, France, and Israel invaded Egypt in October 1956. Using the **Suez crisis** as an excuse, Britain and France took control of the canal but withdrew when Eisenhower would not support them.

Eisenhower then announced the United States would use force to help any nation threatened by communism. This **Eisenhower Doctrine** was used in 1958 to put down a revolt against a pro-American government in Lebanon. The Eisenhower administration also used the **Central Intelligence Agency (CIA)** to help return pro-American governments to Iran and Guatemala.

On October 4, 1957, the Soviets launched the satellite *Sputnik 1.* Alarmed, Congress passed legislation to educate more scientists and created the **National Aeronautics and Space Administration (NASA).**

Review Questions

1. How were brinkmanship and massive retaliation supposed to deter communist aggression?

_____

_____

2. What three countries were the focus of the Eisenhower Doctrine?

_____

_____

READING CHECK

What did each side do to ensure the likelihood of mutually assured destruction?

_____

_____

_____

VOCABULARY STRATEGY

What does the word *perpetual* mean in the underlined sentence? Look at the sentence that comes before it for connections to people and things. Then, look for context clues in the sentence to help you figure out why *perpetual* was used in this sentence.

_____

_____

_____

READING SKILL

Identify Main Ideas Describe the ways the United States and the Soviet Union competed with each other for supremacy.

_____

_____

_____

CHAPTER 16 SECTION 4 — Note Taking Study Guide

THE COLD WAR AT HOME

Focus Question: How did fear of domestic communism affect American society during the Cold War?

A. List efforts taken to protect Americans from communism and how these policies affected rights.

Anticommunist Policy	Effect on Rights

B. As you read, identify similarities and differences between the Hiss case and the Rosenberg case. Consider both the facts and the impact of the two spy cases.

Alger Hiss
- Accused of stealing government documents
- •
- •

- •

Rosenbergs
- Accused of passing on atomic secrets
- •
- •

CHAPTER 16 SECTION 4

Section Summary
THE COLD WAR AT HOME

The **Red Scare**—public fear that communists were working to destroy America both from within and without—spurred President Truman in 1947 to investigate federal employees. About 3,000 people were dismissed or resigned. The Truman administration also used the 1940 **Smith Act,** a law against advocating violent overthrow of the government, to send 11 U.S. Communist Party members to prison.

Meanwhile, the **House Committee on Un-American Activities (HUAC)** investigated subversive activities throughout American life, including academic institutions, labor unions, and city halls. In 1947, HUAC targeted the **Hollywood Ten,** a group of left-wing writers, directors, and producers. They refused to testify against themselves but were sent to prison. Movie executives then circulated a **blacklist** that named entertainment figures suspected of communist ties, shattering many careers.

Two sensational spy trials increased the country's suspicion of communists. The first one concerned **Alger Hiss,** a government employee who had helped organize the United Nations. In 1948, Whittaker Chambers, a former member of the Communist Party and an espionage agent, named Hiss as one of his government contacts. Hiss denied everything before HUAC but was sentenced to five years in prison. The second trial involved **Julius and Ethel Rosenberg,** who were accused of passing secret information about nuclear science to Soviet agents. The Rosenbergs claimed that they were being persecuted because they were Jewish and held unpopular beliefs. They were convicted in a highly controversial trial and executed in 1953.

Joseph R. McCarthy, a senator from Wisconsin, also fanned Americans' fears. He claimed he had a long list of communists in the State Department, but each time he was asked to give specific names and numbers, his figures changed. Still, with the outbreak of the Korean War in 1950, McCarthy's popularity soared. **McCarthyism** became a catchword for the senator's vicious style of reckless charges. McCarthy's targets grew bigger, and in 1954, he went after the United States Army. After viewers saw him badger witnesses and twist the truth during televised hearings, he lost his strongest supporters. The end of the Korean War in 1953 and McCarthy's downfall in 1954 signaled the decline of the Red Scare.

Review Questions

1. How were the Smith Act and HUAC supposed to discourage communism in the United States?

_____

_____

2. What events led to the decline of the Red Scare?

_____

_____

READING CHECK

What happened to the Hollywood Ten?

_____

_____

_____

VOCABULARY STRATEGY

What does the word *academic* mean in the underlined sentence? Use context clues and your prior knowledge to help you figure out what *academic* means.

_____

_____

_____

READING SKILL

Identify Causes and Effects Discuss the events that led to McCarthyism and the popularity of the senator from Wisconsin.

_____

_____

_____

Name _____ Class _____ Date _____

Focus Question: How did the nation experience recovery and economic prosperity after World War II?

List the problems raised by the shift to a peacetime economy and the steps taken to solve them.

United States After WWII	
Problem	**Solution**
• Returning soldiers need jobs.	• GI Bill
•	•
•	•

CHAPTER 17 SECTION 1

Section Summary

AN ECONOMIC BOOM

The production of military supplies halted at the end of World War II. Millions of Americans initially lost their jobs, but soon the nation experienced the longest period of economic growth in American history.

President Harry Truman brought soldiers home by starting the **demobilization,** or sending home members of the army. To calm fears about the economy, the government passed the law known as the **GI Bill of Rights.** The GI Bill provided veterans with unemployment benefits, financial aid for college, and loans to start businesses. Veterans also received home loans, fueling an upsurge in home construction, which led to explosive growth in the suburbs.

Many veterans started families upon returning home. This **baby boom** peaked in 1957 when 4.3 million babies were born. Between 1940 and 1955, the U.S. population grew by 27 percent.

Soaring demand for consumer products caused skyrocketing prices and inflation. Businesses employed more people to produce goods. The United States soon dominated the world economy, producing nearly 50 percent of the world's total output. However, the inflation rate prompted several trade unions to demand pay increases. When employers refused, millions of workers went on strike. Congress then enacted the **Taft-Hartley Act** to outlaw the closed shop—a workplace that hired only union members.

By 1951, Truman's executive order to desegregate the military had been mostly implemented. However, his support of civil rights caused Southern Democrats to leave the party and establish the States' Rights Party. Another split in the Democratic Party led to the creation of the new Progressive Party. The splits seemed to give the 1948 presidential election to Republican Candidate Thomas Dewey. However, Truman won by a narrow margin.

After the election, Truman introduced the **Fair Deal,** a program to strengthen New Deal reforms and establish programs such as national health insurance. Most of the Fair Deal failed in Congress.

In 1952, Republican Dwight Eisenhower won the presidency by a landslide. He helped create an interstate highway system and gave financial support to education.

Review Questions

1. What is the Taft-Hartley Act? Why was it passed?

_____

_____

2. How did President Truman's late-term legislative efforts compare with those of President Eisenhower?

_____

_____

READING CHECK

How much did the U.S. population grow between 1940 and 1955?

_____

_____

_____

VOCABULARY STRATEGY

What does the word *upsurge* mean in the underlined sentence? The word *decrease* is an antonym of *upsurge*. Use the meaning of the antonym and context clues such as "fueling" and "explosive growth" to help you figure out the meaning of *upsurge*.

_____

_____

_____

READING SKILL

Understand Effects How did the GI Bill benefit the American economy?

_____

_____

_____

Name _____ Class _____ Date _____

Focus Question: What social and economic factors changed American life during the 1950s?

A. *Complete the chart below to capture the main ideas.*

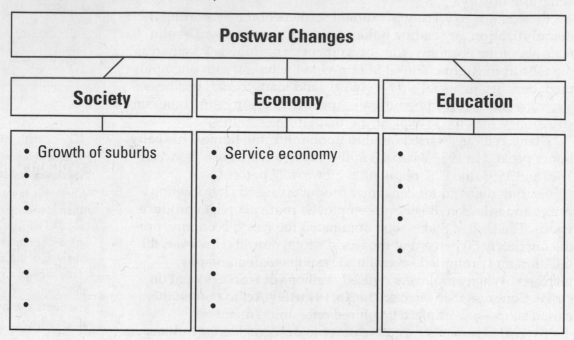

Postwar Changes

Society	Economy	Education
• Growth of suburbs • • • • •	• Service economy • • • • •	• • • •

B. *As you read, identify the effects of the population shift to the Sunbelt.*

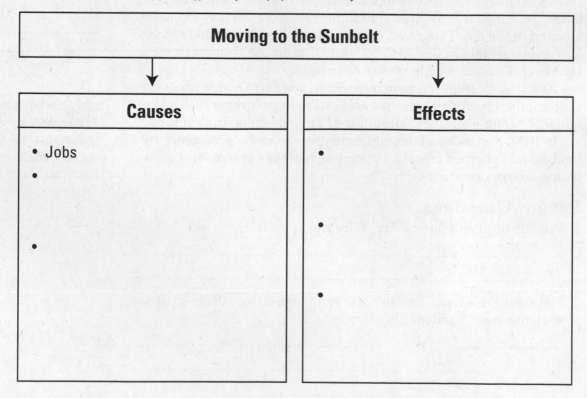

Moving to the Sunbelt

Causes	Effects
• Jobs • •	• • •

CHAPTER
17
SECTION 2

Section Summary
A SOCIETY ON THE MOVE

Between 1940 and 1960, more than 40 million Americans moved to the suburbs, one of the largest mass migrations in history. Developers began quickly building affordable housing in the suburbs to fill the gap left by a shortage of urban housing. Government-backed low-interest loans enabled more people to purchase homes.

Suburban growth would not have been possible had Congress not passed the **Interstate Highway Act** in 1956. This act authorized funds to build 41,000 miles of highway, consisting of multilane expressways that would connect the nation's major cities. The new highways eased the commute from suburbs to cities and boosted the travel and vacation industries.

Southern and western states, known as the **Sunbelt,** also experienced rapid growth. These states had appealing climates and a large number of jobs in the defense, aerospace, and electronics industries. As people moved, their political power moved with them. The Sunbelt and suburbs gained representation while urban areas in the Northeast and the Midwest lost political power.

The American economy was also shifting. Fewer people worked in manufacturing or farming. Employment grew in the **service sector,** businesses that provided services rather than manufactured goods, and **information industries,** businesses that provided informational services. **Franchise businesses** allowed companies to distribute their products and services through retail outlets owned by independent operators. **Multinational corporations,** companies that produced and sold their goods and services across the globe, thrived.

Unions also experienced change. The AFL and the CIO joined in 1955 to form the **AFL-CIO,** bringing them more political clout. However, new white-collar workers generally did not join unions.

Educational opportunities grew as well. By the early 1960s, close to 40 percent of college-age Americans attended college, up from about 15 percent in 1940. The federal government increased education funds, in part to produce more scientists and science teachers. Many states undertook improvement of their public universities. Accessibility to ordinary Americans also increased. California created a **California Master Plan,** creating three tiers of higher education: research universities, state colleges, and community colleges.

Review Questions

1. Discuss the factors that fostered suburban growth.

_____

_____

2. What industries and types of businesses saw job growth in the postwar period?

_____

_____

Why did people move to the Sunbelt?

_____

_____

_____

VOCABULARY STRATEGY

What does *undertook* mean in the underlined sentence? Read the underlined sentence aloud but leave out the word *undertook*. Think about what word you could use in its place. Use this strategy to help you figure out the meaning of *undertook*.

_____

_____

_____

READING SKILL

Identify Main Ideas Discuss changes in American education in the postwar period.

_____

_____

_____

CHAPTER 17 SECTION 3

Note Taking Study Guide

MASS CULTURE AND FAMILY LIFE

Focus Question: How did popular culture and family life change during the 1950s?

Identify postwar changes in daily life and popular culture.

I. **The Culture of Consumerism**
   A. Americans spend more
      1. Increased family income
      2. _____
   B. _____
      1. _____
      2. _____

II. _____
   A. _____
      1. _____
      2. _____
   B. _____
      1. _____
      2. _____
   C. _____
      1. _____
      2. _____
   D. _____
      1. _____
      2. _____

III. _____
   A. _____
   B. _____

IV. _____
   A. _____
   B. _____
      1. _____
      2. _____

CHAPTER 17 SECTION 3

Section Summary

MASS CULTURE AND FAMILY LIFE

As the U.S. economy began to boom in the postwar era, Americans were caught up in a wave of **consumerism**, buying as much as they could, much of it on credit. **Median family income** refers to average family income. Median family income rose dramatically during the 1950s. With money to spend, easy credit, and new goods to buy, shopping became a new pastime for Americans.

During the 1950s, the ideal family was one in which men worked and women stayed home. Popular magazines of the era described the **nuclear family,** or a household consisting of a mother and father and their children, as the backbone of American society. Nevertheless, as the 1950s progressed, more women were willing to challenge the view that a woman should not have a career.

More so than in the past, family life revolved around children. Dr. **Benjamin Spock,** a best-selling author of the era, emphasized the importance of nurturing children, from their earliest days as infants through their teen years. Parents were also spending more money on their children. Some parents even defended their spending by arguing that it would prevent the recurrence of economic depression.

The 1950s also witnessed a revival of religion in the United States. Regular church attendance rose. At the same time, numerous advances in medicine were made, including the widespread use of antibiotics to help control many infectious diseases.

Television had a profound impact on American society, particularly among children. Sitcoms, which rarely discussed real-life problems, were popular. These shows reflected and reinforced the ideal of the 1950s family. Television also eroded distinct regional and ethnic cultures, helping to develop a national culture.

Like television, **rock-and-roll** captured the attention of Americans. Rock music originated in the rhythm and blues traditions of African Americans. **Elvis Presley** made rock music popular when he integrated African American gospel tunes into the music he played. Although some Americans complained about rock music, it nonetheless became a symbol of the emerging youth culture and of the growing power of youth on mass culture.

Review Questions

1. Why did shopping become a new pastime for Americans?

_____

_____

2. Who was Dr. Benjamin Spock?

_____

_____

READING CHECK

Name the medical advancement that helped control infectious diseases.

_____

_____

_____

VOCABULARY STRATEGY

What does the word *nevertheless* mean in the underlined sentence? Circle any words or phrases in the paragraph that help you figure out what *nevertheless* means.

_____

_____

_____

READING SKILL

Identify Main Ideas How did television and rock-and-roll impact postwar American society?

_____

_____

_____

CHAPTER 17
SECTION 4

Note Taking Study Guide
DISSENT AND DISCONTENT

Focus Question: Why were some groups of Americans dissatisfied with conditions in postwar America?

Record the main ideas and supporting details.

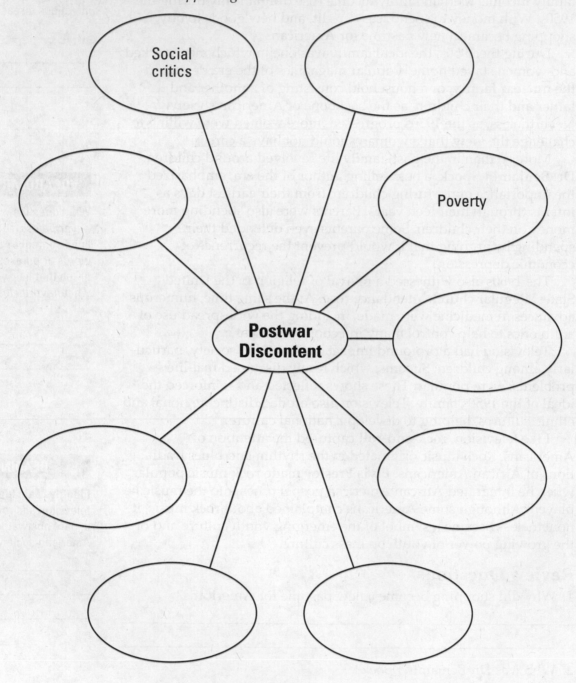

CHAPTER 17 SECTION 4

Section Summary
DISSENT AND DISCONTENT

Despite the prosperity of the 1950s, not everyone benefited from it. Some Americans were dissatisfied with the changes brought by affluence. Social critics and a small group of writers and artists known as **beatniks** criticized what they viewed as the crass materialism and conformity of the American middle class. The theme of alienation, or the feeling of being cut off from mainstream society, dominated many of the era's popular novels.

Hidden behind this prosperity were urban slums, desperate rural poverty, and discrimination. Michael Harrington's influential book *The Other America* (1962) opened America's eyes to the fifty million people, one fourth of the nation, living in poverty. Many of the "invisible" poor were inner-city African Americans, rural whites, and Hispanics in migrant farm camps and urban barrios.

As the middle class moved from cities to the suburbs, cities lost revenue and political clout. Minorities moved in great numbers to cities in search of better economic opportunities. Strained city services such as garbage removal deteriorated. Crime increased in what was now called the **inner city,** further encouraging middle-class Americans to flee. Government-funded **urban renewal** projects tried to reverse this trend by creating developments they hoped would revitalize downtowns. Many failed, pushing people from their homes into already overcrowded areas. To ease the overcrowding and provide affordable housing, the federal government constructed public housing, often in poor neighborhoods. Poverty and associated problems such as crime became further concentrated.

Many of the rural poor also relocated to cities. Small farmers slipped into poverty when they could not compete with the corporations and large-farm owners dominating farm production.

Efforts to overcome housing and employment discrimination became central to the struggle for civil rights. Latinos and Native Americans struggled with many of the same problems. In 1953, the federal government enacted the **termination policy,** a law that sought to end tribal government and to relocate Native Americans to the nation's cities. Proponents of the policy argued that it would free American Indians to assimilate into American society.

Review Questions

1. List three problems that many minorities faced in the postwar era.

_____

_____

2. Discuss how cities changed during this period.

_____

_____

READING CHECK

Who were the beatniks?

_____

_____

_____

VOCABULARY STRATEGY

What does the word *affluence* mean in the underlined sentence? The terms *prosperity* and *material comfort* are synonyms of *affluence.* Use the synonyms to help you figure out the meaning of *affluence.*

_____

_____

_____

READING SKILL

Identify Main Ideas Why did government efforts fail to improve life for minorities?

_____

_____

_____

CHAPTER 18 SECTION 1

Note Taking Study Guide

EARLY DEMANDS FOR EQUALITY

Focus Question: How did African Americans challenge segregation after World War II?

Fill in the timeline below with events of the early civil rights movement. When you finish, write two sentences that summarize the information in your timeline.

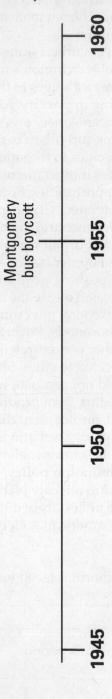

1960

Montgomery
bus boycott

1955

1950

1945

_____

_____

CHAPTER 18 SECTION 1

Section Summary

EARLY DEMANDS FOR EQUALITY

After World War II, Jim Crow laws in the South continued to enforce strict separation of the races. Segregation that is imposed by law is known as **de jure segregation.** African Americans faced segregation in the North, too, even where there were no explicit laws. **De facto segregation,** or segregation by unwritten custom, was a fact of life.

Thurgood Marshall, an African American lawyer, worked with civil rights organizations to challenge segregation in the courts. In 1954, *Brown* v. *Board of Education* challenged segregated public education at all grade levels. Chief Justice **Earl Warren** wrote the *Brown* decision in which the Supreme Court agreed that segregated public schools violated the United States Constitution. The *Brown* decision overturned the principle of "separate but equal." It also lent support to the view that all forms of segregation were wrong.

In Little Rock, Arkansas, the governor ordered the National Guard to block nine African American students from entering the high school. President Eisenhower sent federal troops to protect the students and to enforce the Court's decision. However, southern states continued to resist compliance with the law.

Congress passed the **Civil Rights Act of 1957.** This act established the U.S. Civil Rights Commission. The law's main significance was that it was the first civil rights bill passed by Congress since Reconstruction. It was a small, but important, victory.

In 1955, in Montgomery, Alabama, an African American woman named **Rosa Parks** refused to give up her bus seat to a white passenger. She was arrested. A core of civil rights activists in Montgomery organized a one-day bus boycott to express opposition to Park's arrest and to segregation in general.

The next evening, Dr. **Martin Luther King, Jr.,** a Baptist minister, gave an inspirational speech in which he called upon African Americans to protest segregation and oppression in a nonviolent manner. The **Montgomery bus boycott** continued for more than a year. In 1956, the Supreme Court ruled that the Montgomery city law that segregated buses was unconstitutional. The boycott revealed the power African Americans could have if they joined together. It also helped King and his philosophy of nonviolence to gain prominence within the civil rights movement.

Review Questions

1. Explain the importance of *Brown* v. *Board of Education*.

_____

_____

2. How did the Montgomery bus boycott strengthen the civil rights movement?

_____

_____

READING CHECK

What action did the governor of Arkansas take to prevent the desegregation of schools in Little Rock?

_____

_____

_____

VOCABULARY BUILDER

What does the word *compliance* mean in the underlined sentence? Here is a clue: an antonym for *compliance* is *disobedience.* Use this clue to figure out what *compliance* means.

_____

_____

_____

READING SKILL

Summarize List three key events of the 1950s that helped to end segregation.

_____

_____

_____

Name _____ Class _____ Date _____

Focus Question: How did the civil rights movement gain ground in the 1960s?

Use the concept web below to record information about the civil rights protests of the 1960s.

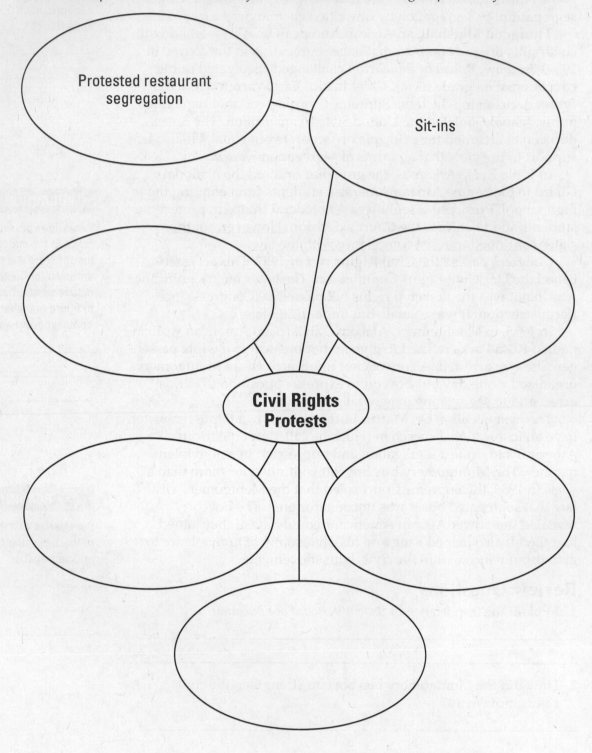

Protested restaurant segregation

Sit-ins

Civil Rights Protests

CHAPTER 18 SECTION 2

Section Summary

THE MOVEMENT GAINS GROUND

Despite some victories, activists continued to struggle for civil rights for African Americans. In North Carolina, four college students started a **sit-in** to protest discrimination. This sit-in sparked a wave of similar protests across the nation. Young African American activists established the **Student Nonviolent Coordinating Committee,** or **SNCC,** to create a grass-roots movement to gain equality.

The next battleground was interstate transportation. The Supreme Court had ruled that segregation on interstate buses was illegal. In the spring of 1961, the Congress of Racial Equality (CORE) staged a **"freedom ride"** through the Deep South to test the federal government's willingness to enforce the law. After the freedom riders met with violence, President John F. Kennedy intervened. Mississippi's leaders agreed to send police to protect the riders.

In September 1962, **James Meredith** won a federal court case that allowed him to enroll at the all-white University of Mississippi. Civil rights activist **Medgar Evers** was instrumental in this effort. Although full-scale riots erupted the night before his arrival, Meredith went on to graduate from the university in 1963.

In the spring of 1963, Martin Luther King, Jr., and the Southern Christian Leadership Conference (SCLC) targeted Birmingham, Alabama, for a major civil rights campaign. The campaign began nonviolently with protest marches and sit-ins. <u>However, Birmingham's Public Safety Commissioner refused to tolerate the demonstrations.</u> He used police dogs and fire hoses on the peaceful protesters. News coverage of the violence shocked many Americans.

To put pressure on Congress to pass a new civil rights bill, supporters organized a massive demonstration in Washington, D.C. More than 200,000 Americans gathered for the **March on Washington** on August 28, 1963. The highlight of the day came when King gave his "I Have a Dream" speech.

On November 22, 1963, President Kennedy was assassinated. Vice President Lyndon B. Johnson assumed the presidency. Johnson used his political skills to gain the passage of the **Civil Rights Act of 1964,** which banned segregation in public accommodations. The surge in support for the civil rights movement had produced a dramatic shift in race relations and set the stage for future reforms.

Review Questions

1. What was the purpose of the March on Washington?

_____

_____

2. Describe the Civil Rights Act of 1964.

_____

_____

READING CHECK

What was the highlight of the March on Washington?

_____

_____

_____

VOCABULARY BUILDER

What does the word *tolerate* mean in the underlined sentence? The word *forbid* is an antonym of *tolerate.* It means "to not permit." Use the meaning of *forbid* to figure out the meaning of *tolerate.*

_____

_____

_____

READING SKILL

Summarize Summarize the significance of James Meredith's actions in 1962.

_____

_____

_____

Note Taking Study Guide
NEW SUCCESSES AND CHALLENGES

Focus Question: What successes and challenges faced the civil rights movement after 1964?

Complete the outline below to summarize the contents of this section.

I. Push for Voting Rights

   A. Freedom Summer

   B. _____

II. _____

   A. _____

   B. _____

III. _____

   A. _____

   B. _____

IV. _____

   A. _____

   B. _____

V. _____

   A. _____

   B. _____

CHAPTER 18 SECTION 3

Section Summary

NEW SUCCESSES AND CHALLENGES

Although the civil rights movement had made progress, the southern political system still prevented African Americans from voting. In 1964, the SNCC mounted a major voter registration project, known as **Freedom Summer.** About 1,000 volunteers flooded Mississippi to register African Americans to vote.

In Selma, Alabama, Martin Luther King, Jr., and the SCLC organized a campaign to pressure the government to enact voting rights legislation. The protests climaxed in a series of confrontations, as heavily armed state troopers attacked the marchers. Spurred by the actions of the protesters, Congress passed the **Voting Rights Act** of 1965, which banned literacy tests. Another legal landmark was the **Twenty-fourth Amendment,** ratified in 1964. This amendment banned the poll tax, which had been used to prevent poor African Americans from voting.

Still, for some African Americans, things had not changed much. In many urban areas, anger over continuing discrimination and poverty erupted into violence and race riots. To determine the causes of the riots, President Johnson established the **Kerner Commission.** The commission concluded that long-term racial discrimination was the single most important cause of violence.

The riots coincided with the radicalization of many young urban African Americans. **Malcolm X** was the most well-known African American radical. Malcolm X became the most prominent minister of the **Nation of Islam,** a religious sect that demanded separation of the races. In February 1965, however, he was assassinated.

Many young African Americans considered themselves heirs of Malcolm X and moved away from the principle of nonviolence. SNCC leader Stokely Carmichael thought that African Americans should use their economic and political muscle, which he termed **"black power,"** to gain equality. Not long after, militants formed the Black Panther Party. Almost overnight, the **Black Panthers** became the symbol of young militant African Americans.

On April 4, 1968, Martin Luther King, Jr., was assassinated. In the wake of his murder, Congress passed the Fair Housing Act, which banned discrimination in housing. Although African Americans had made significant gains, the radicalism of the times left a bitter legacy.

Review Questions

1. Explain the significance of the march in Selma.

_____

_____

2. Why did violence erupt in many American cities in the 1960s?

_____

_____

READING CHECK

Which group became the symbol for young militant African Americans?

_____

_____

_____

VOCABULARY BUILDER

What does the word *confrontations* mean in the underlined sentence? Circle any words or phrases in the paragraph that help you figure out what *confrontations* means.

_____

_____

_____

READING SKILL

Summarize Summarize the impact of Malcolm X on the civil rights movement.

_____

_____

_____

Name _____ Class _____ Date _____

Focus Question: How did Kennedy respond to the continuing challenges of the Cold War?

As you read, list the Cold War crises Kennedy faced and the effects of each event.

Cold War Crisis	Result
Bay of Pigs Invasion	• • •
	• • • •
	• • • • •

Name _____ Class _____ Date _____

The 1960 election featured Democrat **John F. Kennedy** and Republican **Richard M. Nixon.** Both were young, energetic, and intelligent. Kennedy won the election narrowly, in part due to an impressive performance in a televised debate.

As President, Kennedy worked to build up the country's armed forces. He wanted a **"flexible response"** defense policy to prepare the United States to fight any size or any type of conflict. He also wanted to prevent the spread of communism in poor nations around the globe. Like previous leaders, Kennedy believed that democracy combined with prosperity would contain or limit communism's spread. Therefore, he created programs like the **Peace Corps,** which sent American volunteers to help developing countries, to improve the Third World politically and economically.

Kennedy's first major challenge came in Cuba. The revolutionary **Fidel Castro** took over Cuba in 1959 and aligned Cuba with the Soviet Union. Eisenhower had planned an invasion of Cuba to overthrow Castro, and Kennedy executed this plan in 1961. A CIA-led force of Cuban exiles invaded Cuba at the **Bay of Pigs invasion.** The invasion failed and probably ended up strengthening Castro's position in Cuba.

Kennedy's next challenge involved the Soviet premier **Nikita Khrushchev,** who demanded that America remove its troops from West Berlin and recognize the divided city. Kennedy refused. Khrushchev then ordered the construction of a wall between East and West Berlin. The **Berlin Wall** became a symbol of the divide between communism and democracy.

When the Soviets began building nuclear missile sites in Cuba in range of East Coast cities, Kennedy faced his third challenge. During the **Cuban missile crisis,** Kennedy demanded that the Soviets remove the missiles. Nuclear war seemed possible. After several tense days, Khrushchev agreed to remove the missiles. The leaders agreed to install a **"hot line"** telephone system between Moscow and Washington, D.C., to improve communication. A year later, in 1963, the United States, Great Britain, and the Soviet Union signed the first nuclear-weapons agreement.

Review Questions

1. Why did the United States want to overthrow Fidel Castro?

_____

_____

2. Why did U.S. leaders feel threatened by missiles in Cuba?

_____

_____

READING CHECK

Who was the leader of the Soviet Union during the Cuban missile crisis?

_____

_____

_____

VOCABULARY STRATEGY

What does the word *aligned* mean in the underlined sentence? Circle any words or phrases in the paragraph that help you figure out what *aligned* means.

_____

_____

_____

READING SKILL

Understand Effects What effects did the Cuban missile crisis have on the Soviet Union and the United States?

_____

_____

CHAPTER 19 SECTION 2

Note Taking Study Guide

KENNEDY'S NEW FRONTIER

Focus Question: What were the goals of Kennedy's New Frontier?

A. *List the characteristics of John F. Kennedy that appealed to the American people.*

The Kennedy Image
• Youthful
•
•
•
•
•

Name _____ Class _____ Date _____

Focus Question: What were the goals of Kennedy's New Frontier?

B. *As you read, identify details of Kennedy's New Frontier program.*

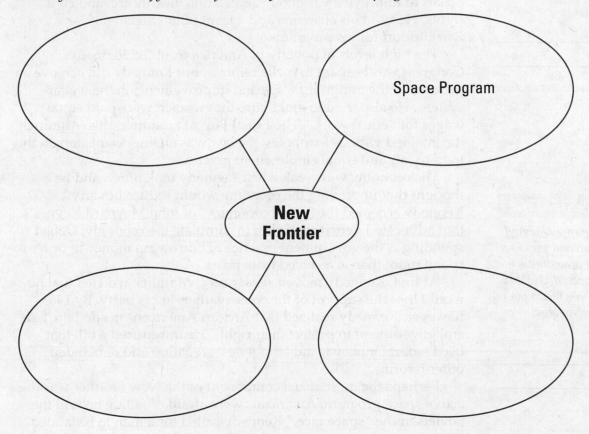

CHAPTER 19 SECTION 2

Section Summary
KENNEDY'S NEW FRONTIER

READING CHECK

What was the job of the Warren Commission?

_____

_____

_____

President Kennedy promised Americans that his administration would blaze a **"New Frontier."** The term described Kennedy's proposals to improve the economy, education, healthcare, and civil rights. He used his charisma and a team of intelligent advisers to win support for his programs.

The high levels of poverty in America troubled Kennedy. Congress was hesitant to make reforms, but Kennedy did achieve an increase in the minimum wage and improvements in the welfare system. He also tried to make sure that women were paid equal wages for "equal work." The **Equal Pay Act** required this. Although it contained various loopholes, the law was an important step on the road to fair and equal employment practices.

The economy was weak when Kennedy took office, and he thought that improving the economy would reduce poverty. Kennedy accepted the "new economics" of John Maynard Keynes that advocated **deficit spending** to stimulate the economy. Deficit spending is the government practice of borrowing money in order to spend more than is received from taxes.

VOCABULARY STRATEGY

What does the word *advocated* mean in the underlined sentence? The word *promoted* is a synonym of *advocated.* Use this synonym to help you figure out the meaning of *advocated.*

_____

_____

_____

At first, Kennedy moved slowly on civil rights, worried that he would lose the support of the conservatives in his party. By 1963, however, Kennedy realized that African Americans needed the federal government to protect their rights. He introduced a bill that used federal money to aid school desegregation and demanded other reforms.

Perhaps the most visual component of the New Frontier was the active space program. Americans were afraid of falling behind the Soviets in the **"space race."** Kennedy called for a man to be landed on the moon in less than 10 years. The goal was met in 1969.

Kennedy's term as President was ended by his assassination. Lee Harvey Oswald shot Kennedy while he was riding in a car in Dallas, Texas. Although many people questioned whether Oswald acted alone, the **Warren Commission,** which conducted the official investigation of the shooting, declared that Oswald acted alone. The senseless murder deeply saddened Americans across the nation. It seemed as if part of America's innocence had died with Kennedy.

READING SKILL

Identify Main Ideas What was deficit spending and why did Kennedy support it?

_____

_____

_____

Review Questions

1. Why did Kennedy want a change in the minimum wage?

_____

_____

2. What did Kennedy do to advance the space program?

_____

_____

CHAPTER 19 SECTION 3

Note Taking Study Guide

JOHNSON'S GREAT SOCIETY

Focus Question: How did Johnson's Great Society programs change life for most Americans?

Identify details about the Great Society programs.

The Great Society			
Education	**Healthcare**	**Immigration**	**Poverty**
•	• Medicare	•	•
•	•		•
			•
			•

CHAPTER 19 SECTION 3

Section Summary
JOHNSON'S GREAT SOCIETY

What programs did Johnson create to fight poverty?

_____

_____

_____

What does the word *outcome* mean in the underlined sentence? Circle any words or phrases in the paragraph that help you figure out what *outcome* means.

_____

_____

_____

Identify Main Ideas What did the Civil Rights Act accomplish?

_____

_____

_____

Lyndon B. Johnson, who became President after Kennedy's assassination, shared the same goals as his predecessor. Johnson's rise to the top was not easy. He was born in a small town in Texas. After attending a state college, he taught in a poor, segregated school for Mexican Americans. After teaching for several years, he was elected to Congress and began working his way up.

Johnson proved to be an excellent politician. One of his first successes after becoming President was ensuring that Congress passed the **Civil Rights Act,** an important bill introduced by President Kennedy. The outcome of this bill was an end to discrimination in voting, education, and public accommodations.

The **War on Poverty** was a big part of Johnson's plans. He wanted to provide more training, education, and healthcare to those who needed it. The **Economic Opportunity Act** began this process by creating agencies such as Job Corps, VISTA, and Head Start.

After being elected President in 1964, Johnson called his vision for America the **Great Society.** He said the Great Society demanded "an end to poverty and racial injustice." In 1965, Congress began to pass Johnson's Great Society legislation.

One area of reform was in healthcare insurance. Johnson created **Medicare,** a program that provided basic hospital insurance for older Americans. He also created **Medicaid,** which provided basic medical services to poor and disabled Americans.

Education and immigration policy also saw reforms. The 1965 Elementary and Secondary Education Act aided schools in poorer communities. The **Immigration and Nationality Act of 1965** relaxed the nation's immigration policies. Over the next two decades, millions of immigrants poured into the United States.

During the 1960s, the Supreme Court was also interested in reform. The court decided cases on controversial social, religious, and political issues. Led by Chief Justice Earl Warren—and often called the **Warren Court**—this liberal court supported civil rights, civil liberties, voting rights, and personal privacy.

Review Questions

1. What did Johnson say was necessary for America to be the Great Society?

_____

_____

2. What is Medicaid?

_____

_____

Name _____ Class _____ Date _____

Note Taking Study Guide
ORIGINS OF THE VIETNAM WAR

Focus Question: Why did the United States become involved in Vietnam?

As you read, describe the Vietnam policies of Presidents Truman, Eisenhower, Kennedy, and Johnson.

U.S. Policy in Vietnam		
Truman/Eisenhower	**Kennedy**	**Johnson**
•	•	•
•	•	•
•		• Gulf of Tonkin Resolution

Name _____ Class _____ Date _____

Who were the Vietcong?

_____

_____

_____

What does the word *ensure* mean in the underlined sentence? Circle any words in the surrounding sentences that could help you learn what *ensure* means.

_____

_____

_____

Summarize Why did the United States help France in Vietnam?

_____

_____

_____

France had controlled Vietnam as a colony since the 1800s. After World War II, however, a strong independence movement took hold. The movement was led by **Ho Chi Minh,** who had been fighting for Vietnamese independence for 30 years. Ho Chi Minh had fled Vietnam in 1912. During his travels around the world, he embraced communism and had formed ties with the Soviet Union.

The United States became involved in Vietnam for several reasons. First, it wanted to keep France as an ally. To ensure French support in the Cold War, President Truman agreed to help France regain control over Vietnam. Second, both Truman and Eisenhower wanted to contain the spread of communism. They believed in the **domino theory.** This idea held that if Vietnam fell to communism, its closest neighbors would follow. Communism would then spread throughout the entire region.

Despite billions of U.S. dollars in support, France lost its hold on Vietnam. In 1954, French troops were trapped at a military base at **Dien Bien Phu.** After 56 days, the French surrendered. At a peace conference in Geneva, Switzerland, France granted independence to Vietnam. The Geneva Accords divided the country into North Vietnam and South Vietnam. Ho Chi Minh's communist forces took power in the north, and an anticommunist government, supported by the United States, ruled in the south.

The United States channeled aid to South Vietnam through the **Southeast Asia Treaty Organization (SEATO).** However, a communist rebel group was determined to undermine the government. Communist guerrilla fighters, called **Vietcong,** were supplied by communists in North Vietnam. They attacked South Vietnamese government officials and destroyed roads and bridges.

In 1961, President Kennedy began sending U.S. troops to South Vietnam. President Johnson increased U.S. involvement after North Vietnam attacked a U.S. destroyer patrolling the Gulf of Tonkin. Congress passed the **Gulf of Tonkin Resolution,** which gave Johnson the authority to use force to defend American troops. This resolution gave the President the power to commit U.S. troops to fight without asking Congress for a formal declaration of war.

Review Questions

1. What was the domino theory?

_____

_____

2. How did the Gulf of Tonkin Resolution expand the powers of the presidency?

_____

_____

Name _____ Class _____ Date _____

Focus Question: What were the causes and effects of America's growing involvement in the Vietnam War?

As you read, fill in the outline with details about the escalation of the American war effort.

I. "Americanizing" the War

    A. _____

        1. _____

        2. _____

    B. _____

        1. _____

        2. _____

    C. _____

        1. _____

        2. _____

II. _____

    A. _____

        1. _____

        2. _____

    B. _____

        1. _____

        2. _____

    C. _____

        1. _____

        2. _____

III. _____

    A. _____

        1. _____

        2. _____

    B. _____

        1. _____

        2. _____

Name _____ Class _____ Date _____

CHAPTER

20

SECTION 2

Section Summary

U.S. INVOLVEMENT GROWS

Which group in Congress opposed the war in Vietnam?

_____

_____

_____

VOCABULARY STRATEGY

What does the word *doctrine* mean in the underlined sentence? Circle the words in the surrounding sentences that could help you learn what *doctrine* means.

_____

_____

_____

READING SKILL

Identify Supporting Details
Why did President Johnson raise taxes?

_____

_____

_____

In February 1965, President Johnson took the United States deeper into the Vietnam War by ordering a large bombing campaign called Operation Rolling Thunder. Despite massive and sustained airstrikes, communist forces continued to fight. Johnson then ordered more troops to fight them on the ground. This more active strategy came primarily from Secretary of Defense Robert McNamara and General **William Westmoreland,** the American commander in South Vietnam.

In addition to conventional bombs, American pilots dropped napalm and sprayed Agent Orange. **Napalm** is a jellied gasoline that covered large areas in flames. Agent Orange is an herbicide that destroys plant life. It was used to disrupt the enemy's food supply.

When the U.S. troops fought on the ground, it was rarely in large battles. The Vietcong and North Vietnamese Army fought with guerrilla tactics in the jungle, trying to wear the United States down because they knew they could not win a traditional war. They followed Ho Chi Minh's doctrine, which stated that fighting should never be on the opponents' terms. Communist forces used hit-and-run attacks, nighttime ambushes, and booby traps. It was also difficult for the U.S. troops to know which Vietnamese person was a friend or an enemy.

By 1967, the war had become a stalemate. By 1968, more than 30,000 Americans had been killed in Vietnam. Despite the many times Johnson asserted that victory was near, each year yielded little progress. Troop morale began to fall.

The costs of the war had also grown each year, straining government finances. Government spending had lowered the unemployment rate at home, but it had also led to rising prices and inflation. President Johnson was forced to raise taxes, and social programs at home had to be cut.

The war was being questioned in Congress, as well. In 1967, Congress was divided into two camps: hawks and doves. **Hawks** supported the war and believed they were fighting communism. **Doves** questioned the war on moral and strategic grounds. They were not convinced that Vietnam was a vital Cold War battleground.

Review Questions

1. Why did President Johnson commit more troops to fight on the ground in Vietnam?

_____

_____

2. What tactics did the communist forces use against U.S. troops in Vietnam?

_____

_____

CHAPTER 20 SECTION 3

Note Taking Study Guide

THE WAR DIVIDES AMERICA

Focus Question: How did the American war effort in Vietnam lead to rising protests and social divisions back home?

Note the events leading up to the 1968 election.

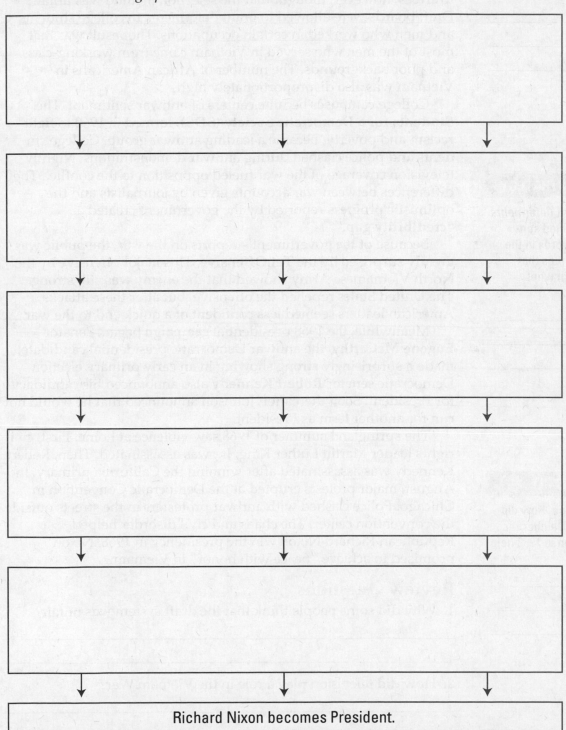

Richard Nixon becomes President.

CHAPTER 20 SECTION 3

Section Summary
THE WAR DIVIDES AMERICA

VOCABULARY STRATEGY

What does the word *deferments* mean in the underlined sentence? Circle the words in the surrounding sentences that could help you learn what *deferments* means.

_____

_____

_____

READING SKILL

Recognize Sequence How did the protests at the Democratic National Convention in 1968 help Richard Nixon?

_____

_____

_____

The war in Vietnam divided Americans and opened a deep emotional rift in American society. To provide enough soldiers for the war, the government drafted young men into service. Some of these **draftees,** however, thought that the selection method was unfair. Draft boards were allowed to grant deferments to college students and men who worked in certain occupations. The result was that most of the men who served in Vietnam came from working-class and poor backgrounds. The number of African Americans in Vietnam was also disproportionately high.

College campuses became centers of antiwar sentiment. The **Students for a Democratic Society (SDS),** formed in 1960 to fight racism and poverty, became a leading antiwar group. College students and police clashed during antiwar demonstrations. Nightly television coverage of the war fueled opposition to the conflict. The differences between war accounts given by journalists and the optimistic progress reported by the government created a **"credibility gap."**

Because of the government's reports on the war, the public was greatly surprised by the **Tet Offensive.** This major offensive by the North Vietnamese Army showed that the enemy was still strong. The United States repelled the offensive, but after these attacks, American leaders seemed less confident of a quick end to the war.

Meanwhile, the 1968 presidential campaign began. Senator **Eugene McCarthy,** the antiwar Democratic presidential candidate, made a surprisingly strong showing in an early primary election. Democratic senator **Robert Kennedy** also announced his candidacy for President. Soon thereafter, Johnson announced that he would not run for another term as President.

The spring and summer of 1968 saw violence at home. First, civil rights leader Martin Luther King, Jr., was assassinated. Then, Robert Kennedy was assassinated after winning the California primary. In August, major protests erupted at the Democratic Convention in Chicago. Police clashed with antiwar protesters in the streets outside the convention center. The chaos and civil disorder helped Republican Richard Nixon win the presidency in 1968. Nixon promised to achieve "peace with honor" in Vietnam.

Review Questions

1. Why did some people think that the draft system was unfair?

_____

_____

2. How did television play a role in the Vietnam War?

_____

_____

Name _____ Class _____ Date _____

Focus Question: How did the Vietnam War end, and what were its lasting effects?

A. *Note the similarities and differences between Nixon's Vietnam policy and that of Lyndon Johnson.*

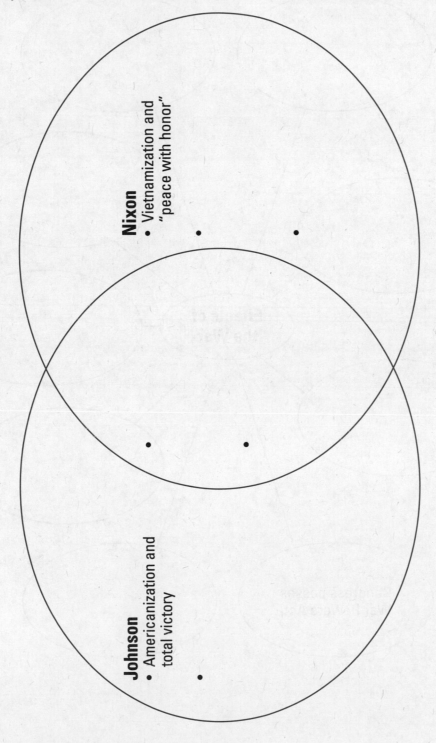

Nixon
• Vietnamization and "peace with honor"

Johnson
• Americanization and total victory

CHAPTER
20
SECTION 4

Note Taking Study Guide
THE WAR'S END AND IMPACT

Focus Question: How did the Vietnam War end, and what were its lasting effects?

B. *As you read, use the concept web below to identify the effects of the Vietnam War.*

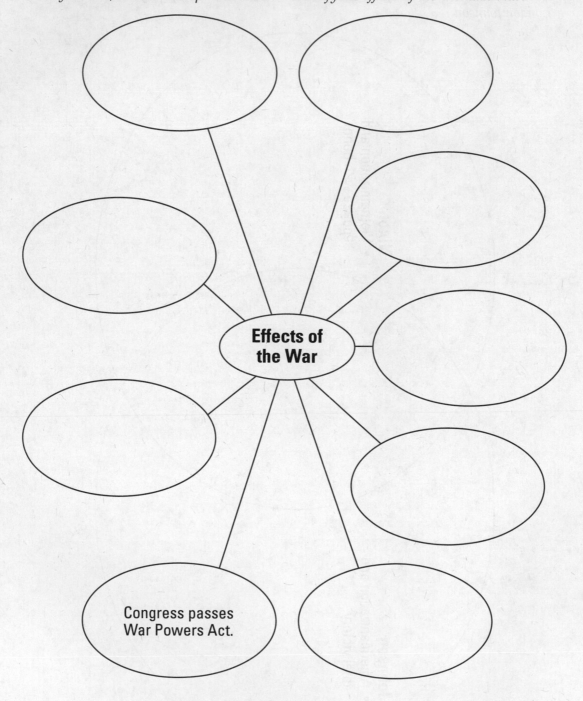

CHAPTER 20 SECTION 4

Section Summary

THE WAR'S END AND IMPACT

When Nixon became President, he believed that a peace deal could be negotiated with North Vietnam. When these negotiations stalled, however, Nixon gradually began to pull American troops out of Vietnam. He believed that the South Vietnamese Army should fight on its own and called this approach **Vietnamization.** He hoped that American supplies to the South Vietnamese Army would be sufficient for the army to secure and hold South Vietnam.

In 1970, however, Nixon ordered a ground attack on communists in Cambodia, which angered antiwar activists at home who claimed that Nixon was widening the war, not ending it. Protests erupted on many college campuses. At **Kent State University,** members of the National Guard fired into a group of protesters, killing four. This led to demonstrations on other campuses, including Jackson State in Mississippi, where two students were killed.

Other events also outraged the public. American troops killed over four hundred unarmed Vietnamese in the village of **My Lai.** The **Pentagon Papers** showed that the government had been dishonest with the public and with Congress about the Vietnam War.

American bombing finally induced the North Vietnamese to resume negotiations. In January 1973, the United States, South Vietnam, North Vietnam, and the Vietcong signed the **Paris Peace Accords.** American troops would withdraw from South Vietnam, and North Vietnamese troops would remain in South Vietnam. The war was over for the United States, but fighting continued in Vietnam. The Soviet-supplied North Vietnamese Army defeated the South Vietnamese Army, and Vietnam was united under a communist regime.

More than 58,000 American troops and over 2 million Vietnamese had been killed in the Vietnam War. Turmoil troubled Southeast Asia for many years afterward. After the difficult experience in Vietnam, Americans were less willing to intervene in the affairs of other countries. Americans had less trust in their leaders, as well. In 1973, Congress passed the **War Powers Act,** which restricted the President's authority to commit American troops to foreign conflicts. The fear of "another Vietnam" would affect American foreign policy for decades to come.

Review Questions

1. What was Vietnamization?

_____

_____

2. Why did the Pentagon Papers outrage Americans?

_____

_____

READING CHECK

How many American troops were killed in Vietnam?

_____

_____

_____

VOCABULARY STRATEGY

What does the word *induced* mean in the underlined sentence? Circle the words in the underlined sentence that could help you learn what *induced* means.

_____

_____

_____

READING SKILL

Recognize Effects What was one effect of the Vietnam War on American foreign policy?

_____

_____

_____

CHAPTER 20 SECTION 5

Note Taking Study Guide

NIXON AND THE COLD WAR

Focus Question: How did Richard Nixon change Cold War diplomacy during his presidency?

As you read, describe Nixon's Cold War foreign policies in dealing with China and the Soviet Union.

Nixon's Cold War Strategies	
China	**Soviet Union**
• Normalization of relations will drive wedge between China and Soviet Union. • •	• Diplomacy with China will create Soviet fear of isolation. • •

CHAPTER 20 SECTION 5

Section Summary

NIXON AND THE COLD WAR

During his years as President, Richard Nixon fundamentally reshaped the way the United States approached the world. His leading adviser on national security and international affairs, **Henry Kissinger,** helped him.

In foreign affairs, Nixon and Kissinger shared the idea of **realpolitik,** a German word meaning "real politics." According to this idea, a nation's political goals around the world should be defined by what is good for the nation instead of by abstract ideologies. <u>Nixon and Kissinger argued that a flexible, pragmatic foreign policy would benefit the United States in many ways.</u>

Nixon had built his career as a strong opponent of communism. Therefore, his first bold move, to normalize relations with China, came as a surprise. In the 1960s, the United States still did not officially recognize communist China. Nixon understood that communist China could not be ignored. He tried to accomplish several goals by reaching out to China. First, he wanted to drive a wedge between China and the Soviet Union. Second, China could be a good trading partner. Third, perhaps China could pressure North Vietnam to accept a negotiated peace and end the Vietnam War. In 1972, Nixon traveled to China and met with Premier **Zhou Enlai** and Chairman Mao Zedong. The visit was a historic first step toward normalizing relations between the two countries.

Nixon's trip to China was met by an immediate reaction from the Soviet Union. Soviet leader Leonid Brezhnev invited the President to visit Moscow, where they signed the first **Strategic Arms Limitation Treaty.** This agreement froze the deployment of intercontinental ballistic missiles and placed limits on antiballistic missiles. The treaty was a first step toward limiting the arms race.

The United States and Soviet Union now implemented a new policy called **détente** to replace the prior foreign policy, which was based on suspicion and distrust. Détente eased tensions between the two nations.

Nixon's foreign policy changed the nation's stance toward communism. In the short term, the new relationships he forged helped to end the Vietnam War. In the long term, his foreign policy moved the world closer to the end of the Cold War.

Review Questions

1. Why did Nixon want to normalize relations with China?

_____

_____

2. What was the effect of détente?

_____

_____

READING CHECK

What is realpolitik?

_____

_____

_____

VOCABULARY STRATEGY

What does the word *pragmatic* mean in the underlined sentence? Circle the words in the underlined sentence that could help you learn what *pragmatic* means.

_____

_____

_____

READING SKILL

Categorize Circle the statement that most accurately reflects President Nixon's attitudes toward communism.

- If Vietnam fell to communism, its closest neighbors would follow, spreading communism throughout the region.

- A flexible, pragmatic foreign policy would benefit the United States in many ways.

- The United States should support all independence movements, no matter what their political beliefs.

Name _____ Class _____ Date _____

Focus Question: What was the counterculture, and what impact did it have on American society?

As you read, use the concept web below to record main ideas about the counterculture.

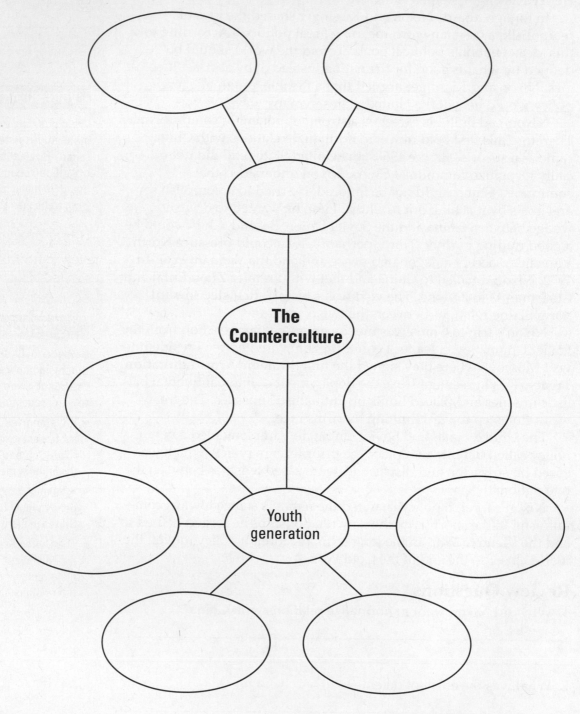

CHAPTER 21 SECTION 1

Section Summary
THE COUNTERCULTURE

The **counterculture** grew out of the Beat movement's emphasis on freedom from materialism and the civil rights movement's questioning of traditional boundaries. The Vietnam antiwar movement's distrust of authority fostered a spirit of rebellion. Members of the counterculture, known as hippies, valued youth, spontaneity, and individuality, and promoted peace, love, and freedom. <u>Their experimentation with drugs, new styles of dress and music, and freer attitudes toward sexual relationships contradicted traditional values and boundaries.</u> This rebellion led to misunderstanding between the older and younger generation, a situation that was called a **generation gap.**

Born after World War II, the younger generation had an enormous influence on American society, driving changes in attitudes and styles in everything from clothes to music and art. Rock-and-roll music by bands such as the **Beatles** came to define the decade. Hippies rejected many traditional restrictions on sexual behavior in what became known as the "sexual revolution." Many also often adopted new living patterns, residing in **communes,** small communities where people shared interests and resources.

The center of the counterculture was the **Haight-Ashbury** district of San Francisco. Here hippies experimented with drugs and listened to rock music and speeches by political radicals such as **Timothy Leary,** who encouraged youths to "tune in," "turn on" to drugs, and "drop out" of mainstream society.

Some hippies sought spirituality outside of the Judeo-Christian tradition, exploring Eastern religions and practices of Native Americans. Some sought to live off the land in harmony with nature. These beliefs impacted the growing environmental movement.

By the late 1960s, several key figures of the counterculture were dead of drug overdoses, and many people had become disillusioned with the movement's excesses. Most hippies eventually rejoined the mainstream, but the seeds of protest sown during the 1960s would influence the growing "rights revolution."

Review Questions

1. How did social and political events help shape the counterculture?

_____

_____

2. In what ways did the counterculture influence American culture?

_____

_____

READING CHECK

What district in San Francisco was at the center of the counterculture?

_____

_____

_____

VOCABULARY STRATEGY

What does the word *contradicted* mean in the underlined sentence? Circle the words in the underlined sentence that could help you learn what *contradicted* means.

_____

_____

_____

READING SKILL

Identify Main Ideas The counterculture's music, art, and style of dress reflected a rejection of what aspect of society?

_____

_____

_____

Note Taking Study Guide

CHAPTER 21 SECTION 2

THE WOMEN'S RIGHTS MOVEMENT

Focus Question: What led to the rise of the women's movement, and what impact did it have on American society?

Record the causes, effects, and main figures in the women's movement in the chart below.

The Women's Movement		
Causes	**Proponents/ Opponents**	**Effects**
•	•	•
•	•	•
•	•	•
•		

CHAPTER
21
SECTION 2

Section Summary
THE WOMEN'S RIGHTS MOVEMENT

The first wave of feminism began in the 1840s and culminated in 1920 with women winning the right to vote. **Feminism** is the theory of political, social, and economic equality for men and women. The second wave of feminism was born in the 1960s. Inspired by successes of the civil rights movement, women wanted to change how they were treated as a group and to redefine how they were viewed as individuals.

The role of housewife was seen as the proper one for women, but many women found it deeply unsatisfying. Those women who did work experienced open and routine discrimination, including being paid less than men. **Betty Friedan** described women's dissatisfaction in her 1963 book *The Feminine Mystique.* Friedan later helped establish the **National Organization for Women (NOW),** which sought to win equality for women. The group campaigned for passage of the **Equal Rights Amendment (ERA),** an amendment to the Constitution that would guarantee gender equality under the law. NOW also worked to protect a woman's right to an abortion. Radical feminists went further, conducting protests to expose discrimination against women. One radical feminist was **Gloria Steinem,** who sought to raise consciousness through the media and helped co-found *Ms.* magazine in 1972.

Not all women supported these efforts. **Phyllis Schlafly,** a conservative political activist, denounced women's liberation as "a total assault on the family, on marriage, and on children." The ERA failed to pass partly due to her efforts.

Women did, however, gain new legal rights. Title IX of the Higher Education Act of 1972 banned discrimination in education and the Equal Credit Opportunity Act made it illegal to deny credit to a woman on the basis of gender. The 1973 Supreme Court decision in *Roe* v. *Wade* gave women the right to legal abortions.

Changes in the workplace came slowly. Today, more women work, and more work in fields such as medicine and law that were once limited to them. Despite these gains, the average woman still earns less than the average man, partly because women continue to work in fields that pay less.

Review Questions

1. What was the goal of the Equal Rights Amendment?

_____

_____

2. What causes did the National Organization for Women work toward? Did its efforts succeed or fail?

_____

_____

READING CHECK

Who founded *Ms.* magazine?

_____

_____

_____

VOCABULARY STRATEGY

What does the word *gender* mean in the underlined sentence? Look for context clues in the sentence and surrounding sentences to help you identify what *gender* refers to.

_____

_____

_____

READING SKILL

Identify Causes and Effects
What inspired the second wave of feminism?

_____

_____

_____

Name _____ Class _____ Date _____

Focus Question: How did the rights movements of the 1960s and 1970s expand rights for diverse groups of Americans?

A. *Compare and contrast the Latino and Native American rights movements in the Venn diagram below.*

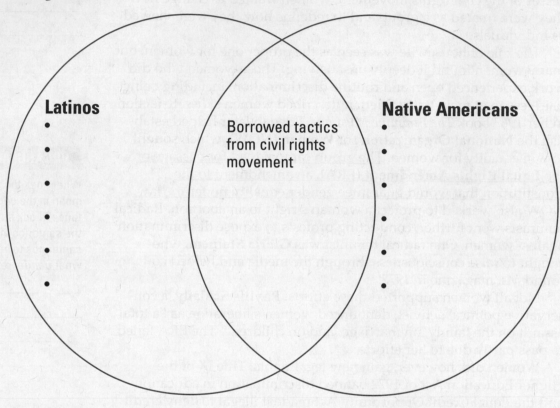

Latinos

-
-
-
-
-
-
-

Borrowed tactics from civil rights movement

Native Americans

-
-
-
-
-
-

B. *As you read, identify causes of expanding rights for consumers and those with disabilities.*

Consumer Advocacy	Disabled Advocacy
• •	• •

↓ ↓

Growing Movements Expand Rights

CHAPTER
21
SECTION 3

Section Summary
THE RIGHTS REVOLUTION EXPANDS

Mexican and other Latin American immigrants came to the United States during and after World War II, filling the need for cheap labor. Mexican immigrants came as temporary farmworkers. Other immigrants came from Puerto Rico, Cuba, and the Dominican Republic. The *bracero* program allowed Mexicans to work on American farms. After passage of the Immigration and Nationality Act Amendments in 1965, immigration from Latin America surged.

Following the lead of the civil rights movement, Latinos began fighting for their rights. The most influential Latino activist was **Cesar Chavez,** who formed the **United Farm Workers (UFW).** This union implemented a strike and boycott of grapes that secured safer working conditions for **migrant farmworkers.** These workers were often exploited as they moved from farm to farm to pick fruits and vegetables. A broader movement known as the **Chicano movement** worked to raise consciousness, reduce poverty and discrimination, and attain political power for Latinos.

Native Americans formed their own protest groups. One group took over the island of Alcatraz and claimed it for the Sioux. Another group, the **American Indian Movement (AIM),** was founded in 1968 to ease poverty and help secure legal rights and self-government for Native Americans. In February 1973, AIM took over Wounded Knee, South Dakota, to protest living conditions on reservations. That protest that led to the deaths of two AIM members. Laws helping Native Americans were passed in the 1970s, including the Indian Self-Determination Act of 1975, which granted tribes greater control over resources on reservations.

The consumer rights movement started after **Ralph Nader** published *Unsafe at Any Speed,* a book that investigated the link between flawed car design and deaths in automobile accidents. The book prompted Congress to pass laws to improve automobile safety. Americans with disabilities, due in part to activism by Korean and Vietnam war veterans, also secured additional rights. Several laws were passed in the 1970s guaranteeing equal access to education for those with disabilities.

Review Questions

1. What factors encouraged Latinos to immigrate to the United States during and after World War II?

_____

_____

2. What changes did those fighting for consumer and disabled rights help bring about?

_____

_____

READING CHECK

What organization did Cesar Chavez help organize?

_____

_____

_____

VOCABULARY STRATEGY

What does the word *implemented* mean in the underlined sentence? Look for clues in the surrounding words, phrases, and sentences. Circle the words in the underlined sentence that could help you learn what *implemented* means.

_____

_____

_____

READING SKILL

Compare and Contrast Compare and contrast the results of the UFW's work and Ralph Nader's book.

_____

_____

_____

CHAPTER
21
SECTION 4

Note Taking Study Guide
THE ENVIRONMENTAL MOVEMENT

Focus Question: What forces gave rise to the environmental movement, and what impact did it have?

As you read, record major events in the environmental movement in the flowchart below.

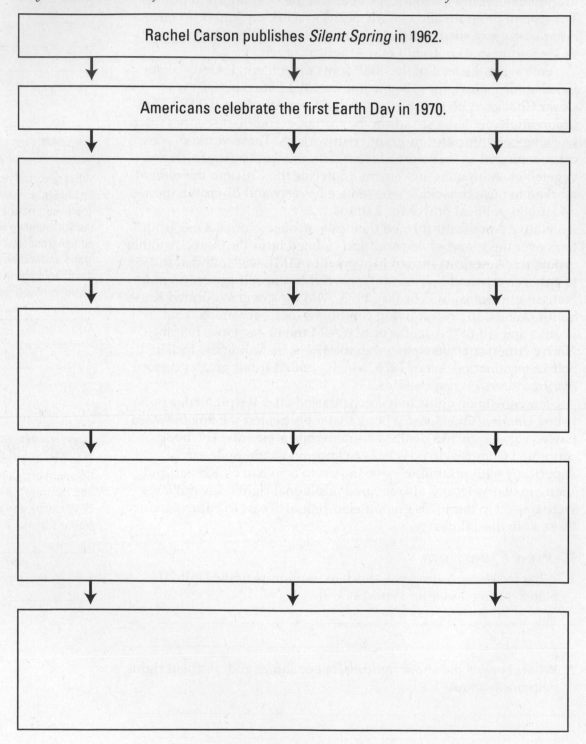

Rachel Carson publishes *Silent Spring* in 1962.

Americans celebrate the first Earth Day in 1970.

CHAPTER 21
SECTION 4

Section Summary
THE ENVIRONMENTAL MOVEMENT

Published in 1962, *Silent Spring,* by **Rachel Carson,** inspired much environmental activism. The book describes the deadly impact that pesticides were having on birds and other animals. Carson argued that humans were drastically altering the environment and had a responsibility to protect it. Protests sparked by the book eventually compelled Congress to restrict use of the pesticide DDT.

Other environmental concerns included **toxic waste** such as coal smog—poisonous byproducts of human activity. One response to environmental concern was **Earth Day.** Close to 20 million Americans took part in the first Earth Day, held on April 22, 1970, and it has since become an annual event.

Public outcry over environmental issues convinced President Nixon to support environmental reforms. Under his leadership, Congress created the **Environmental Protection Agency (EPA)** in 1970 to protect "the entire ecological chain." The EPA worked to clean up and protect the environment and sought to limit or eliminate pollutants that posed a risk to the public's health. Nixon also signed a number of environmental laws. The **Clean Air Act** (1970) combated air pollution by limiting the emissions from factories and automobiles. The **Clean Water Act** (1973) reduced water pollution by industry and agriculture. The **Endangered Species Act** (1973) helped to protect endangered plants and animals.

In the late 1970s, several crises reinforced the public's environmental concern. Toxic waste in the ground was blamed for high rates of birth defects and cancer in Love Canal, New York. Later, a nuclear reactor at Three Mile Island in Pennsylvania malfunctioned and the core began to melt.

While these events solidified some people's support for environmental regulation, other people questioned and opposed the government's actions. Conservatives complained that regulations took away individuals' property rights. Others argued that private property owners rather than the government should protect the environment. Industry leaders worried that too much environmental regulation would harm business.

Review Questions

1. What environmental protection laws were passed during President Nixon's tenure?

_____

_____

2. What arguments did some people make against the U.S. government's role in environmental protection?

_____

_____

READING CHECK

What agency works to limit or eliminate pollution?

_____

_____

_____

VOCABULARY STRATEGY

What does the word *compelled* mean in the underlined sentence? Look for clues in the surrounding words, phrases, and sentences. Circle the word below that is a synonym for *compelled.*

- forced
- voluntary

READING SKILL

Recognize Sequence What people and events influenced President Nixon's environmental reforms?

_____

_____

_____

Name ______________________ Class ________________ Date ________

CHAPTER 22 SECTION 1

Note Taking Study Guide

NIXON AND THE WATERGATE SCANDAL

Focus Question: What events led to Richard Nixon's resignation as President in 1974?

A. *Record Nixon's major domestic policies and goals in the chart below.*

Nixon's Domestic Policies and Strategies	
New Federalism	**Southern Strategy**
•	•
•	•
•	•
•	

B. *Use the chart below to record the causes and effects of the Watergate crisis.*

Watergate Crisis

Causes	Effects
• Break-in at Democratic Party headquarters	• Connections revealed between burglars and White House
•	•
•	•
•	•
•	•

CHAPTER 22 SECTION 1

Section Summary

NIXON AND THE WATERGATE SCANDAL

In 1968, Richard Nixon narrowly defeated Democrat Hubert Humphrey to win the presidency. During the campaign, Nixon claimed to represent the **silent majority,** the working men and women who made up Middle America. He believed that they were tired of "big" government. <u>However, he also believed that they wanted the government to address social problems like crime and pollution.</u> He proposed revenue sharing, in which the federal government gave money to the states to run social programs. He also sponsored programs to regulate workplace safety, to administer the federal war on illegal drugs, and to enforce environmental standards. Nixon's presidency was plagued by a combination of recession and inflation that came to be known as **stagflation.** When the **Organization of Petroleum Exporting Countries (OPEC)** placed an oil embargo on Israel's allies, oil prices skyrocketed.

Nixon set out to expand his base of support. His **southern strategy** targeted southern whites, who had traditionally voted for Democrats. He appointed conservative southern judges and criticized the court-ordered busing of school children to achieve desegregation. However, he also supported new **affirmative action** plans in employment and education. Nixon won the 1972 election easily, becoming the first Republican presidential candidate to sweep the entire South.

In June 1972, burglars broke into the Democratic Party headquarters at the Watergate complex in Washington. After their conviction, one of them charged that administration officials had been involved. Nixon denied any wrongdoing in what came to be known as the **Watergate** scandal. In the fall of 1973, Vice President Agnew resigned in the face of an unrelated corruption scandal. Under the **Twenty-fifth Amendment,** Nixon nominated Gerald Ford to become his new Vice President. Nixon refused to turn over secret tapes of Oval Office conversations. He claimed **executive privilege,** which is the principle that the President has the right to keep certain information confidential. However, the Supreme Court ordered Nixon to turn over the tapes. These tapes provided evidence of Nixon's involvement in the coverup. In order to avoid impeachment and conviction, Nixon resigned in August 1974.

Review Questions

1. What was Richard Nixon's attitude toward "big" government?

_____

_____

2. How did Watergate lead to a showdown between the President and the Supreme Court?

_____

_____

READING CHECK

What was Nixon's southern strategy?

_____

_____

_____

VOCABULARY STRATEGY

What does the word *pollution* mean in the underlined sentence? Look for context clues in the surrounding words, phrases, and sentences. Circle the word below that is a synonym for *pollution.*

• contamination

• purification

READING SKILL

Identify Main Ideas In what areas did Nixon expand the federal government's role?

_____

_____

_____

CHAPTER
22
SECTION 2

Note Taking Study Guide
THE FORD AND CARTER YEARS

Focus Question: What accounted for the changes in American attitudes during the 1970s?

Use the outline below to record the political, economic, and social problems of the era and their impact on American society.

I. Gerald Ford's Presidency

    A. Major Domestic Issues

        1. _____

        2. _____

        3. _____

        4. _____

II. _____

    A. _____

    B. _____

    C. _____

    D. _____

III. _____

    A. _____

    B. _____

    C. _____

    D. _____

    E. _____

Name _____ Class _____ Date _____

Gerald Ford had a long record of public service. When he became President after Nixon's resignation, he had the support of Democrats as well as Republicans. However, he lost support when he announced that he had **pardoned**, or officially forgiven, Nixon for any crimes he might have committed as President. The pardon was meant to heal the nation's wounds, but Ford's critics accused him of having made a secret deal. The 1974 congressional elections showed the public's disapproval of the pardon and the impact of Watergate. The Republicans lost 48 seats in the House of Representatives.

Former Georgia governor **Jimmy Carter** won the presidency in the 1976 election. He was a born-again Christian who won the support of many **Christian fundamentalists.** He also was a Washington outsider who had no close ties with the Democratic leadership in Congress. Most of the bills he submitted to Congress did not pass without major changes by his own party. A day after his inauguration, he granted **amnesty** to Americans who had evaded the draft, in the hope of moving the nation beyond the Vietnam War. Severe inflation continued, fueled by the ongoing energy crisis. Carter contended with the oil crisis by calling on Americans to conserve energy.

The migration of Americans to the Sunbelt and the growth of the suburbs continued during the 1970s. The Sunbelt's political power also grew. An influx of immigrants from Latin America and Asia also occured. The divorce rate more than doubled between 1965 and 1979, and the number of children born out of wedlock nearly tripled. The 1970s are sometimes called the "me decade" because many Americans appeared to be absorbed with self-improvement. This included an increased interest in fitness and health. Millions began to jog and eat natural foods.

The 1970s also witnessed a resurgence of fundamental Christianity. **Televangelists** such as Jerry Falwell preached to millions on television. Religious conservatives opposed many of the social changes begun in the 1960s that had gone mainstream in the 1970s. They began to form alliances with other conservatives to forge a new political majority.

Review Questions

1. What events cast a shadow over Gerald Ford's presidency?

_____

_____

2. How did Jimmy Carter deal with the energy crisis?

_____

_____

READING CHECK

Why were the 1970s called the "me decade"?

_____

_____

_____

VOCABULARY STRATEGY

What does the word *contended* mean in the underlined sentence? Note that the word is a verb. Ask yourself what kind of action President Carter was taking in relation to the oil crisis. Use this strategy to help you figure out what *contended* means.

_____

_____

_____

READING SKILL

Identify Main Ideas How did being an outsider in Washington hurt Carter's presidency?

_____

_____

_____

Name _____ Class _____ Date _____

Focus Question: What were the goals of American foreign policy during the Ford and Carter years, and how successful were Ford's and Carter's policies?

Use the concept web below to record the main ideas and details about the foreign policies of Ford and Carter.

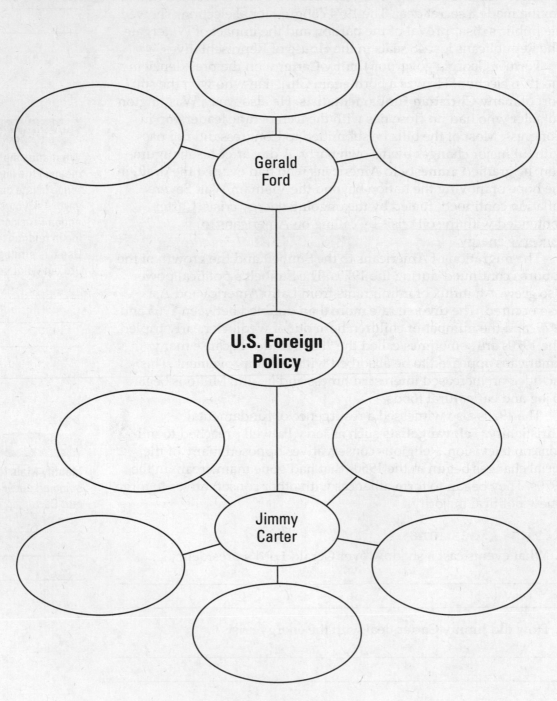

CHAPTER 22 SECTION 3

Section Summary
FOREIGN POLICY TROUBLES

Relations with the Soviet Union were central to U.S. foreign policy during the Ford and Carter administrations. President Gerald Ford and Soviet leader Leonid Brezhnev met twice and endorsed the **Helsinki Accords.** In this document, the nations of Europe expressed their support of **human rights.** However, Ford chose to put arms control ahead of human rights. The United States continued disarmament talks with the Soviets. When South Vietnam fell to the communists, hundreds of thousands of Vietnamese tried to escape in rickety boats. These **boat people** represented the largest mass migration by sea in modern history.

Early in his presidency, Jimmy Carter announced that his foreign policy would be guided by a concern for human rights. He tried to use his foreign policy to end acts of political repression, such as torture. Carter also worked to achieve détente, and in 1979, he signed the **SALT II** treaty to limit nuclear arms production. However, relations between the two superpowers took a frosty turn after the Soviet Union invaded Afghanistan in December 1979. Carter responded by imposing **sanctions** on the Soviets, including a boycott of the 1980 Summer Olympic Games in Moscow. Carter also hoped to change the way the United States dealt with the **developing world.** His emphasis on human rights led him to alter the U.S. relationship with a number of dictators.

Carter's greatest foreign policy success and setback were both in the Middle East. Egypt and Israel had been enemies since Israel's founding in 1948. In 1977, Carter invited the leaders of the two nations to the presidential retreat. The result was the **Camp David Accords,** which led to a peace treaty in which Egypt recognized Israel. In January 1979, the U.S.-backed Shah of Iran was forced to flee. Fundamentalist Islamic clerics, led by the **Ayatollah Khomeini,** took power. Iranian radicals invaded the U.S. Embassy and took 66 Americans hostage. The Khomeini government took control of both the embassy and the hostages to defy the United States. The hostage crisis consumed Carter's attention during his last year in office. His failure to win the release of the hostages was viewed as evidence of American weakness.

Review Questions

1. Compare the foreign policies of Gerald Ford and Jimmy Carter.

_____

_____

2. How did the Iran hostage crisis affect the last year of Carter's presidency?

_____

_____

READING CHECK

Why did the United States boycott the 1980 Summer Olympic Games?

_____

_____

_____

VOCABULARY STRATEGY

What does the word *repression* mean in the underlined sentence? Look for context clues in the surrounding sentences to help you figure out the meaning of *repression.*

_____

_____

_____

READING SKILL

Identify Supporting Details List two details that support the following statement: Carter's greatest foreign policy challenges were in the Middle East.

_____

_____

_____

CHAPTER 23 SECTION 1

Note Taking Study Guide
THE CONSERVATIVE MOVEMENT GROWS

Focus Question: What spurred the rise of conservatism in the late 1970s and early 1980s?

As you read, summarize the rise of the conservative movement in the outline below.

I. Two Views: Liberal and Conservative

   A. Liberal ideas and goals

      1. _____

         _____

      2. _____

         _____

      3. _____

         _____

   B. _____

      _____

      1. _____

         _____

      2. _____

         _____

      3. _____

         _____

CHAPTER 23 SECTION 1

Section Summary
THE CONSERVATIVE MOVEMENT GROWS

The two major political parties in the late twentieth century were the Democrats, many of whom were "liberals," and the Republicans, often labeled "conservatives." **Liberals** believed that the federal government should play an active role in improving the lives of all Americans. They supported social programs and government regulation of industry, and favored cooperation with international organizations such as the United Nations.

Conservatives believed that the free market, private organizations, and individuals, instead of the government, should care for the needy. They opposed big government, favored tax cuts, and supported a strong military.

Many things contributed to the conservative movement known as the **New Right,** which grew rapidly during the 1960s and 1970s. The Vietnam War and urban riots of the 1960s divided the country. The counterculture had alienated many Americans. Watergate, the oil crises of the 1970s, and the Iran hostage crisis further weakened the public's faith in the federal government. When the economy stagnated, conservative beliefs became more attractive.

Conservatives blamed liberal policies for the economic problems of the late 1970s. They believed that the government taxed too heavily and spent too much money on the wrong programs. They complained about **unfunded mandates,** programs required but not paid for by the federal government.

In 1979, Reverend Jerry Falwell founded the **Moral Majority,** a political organization based on religious beliefs. Supporters worried about the decline of the traditional family. They were also concerned that the new freedoms brought by the counterculture would lead to the degeneration of modern youth.

The conservative movement swept the Republican presidential candidate, former actor and two-term California governor **Ronald Reagan,** to victory over Democratic incumbent Jimmy Carter in the 1980 election. Reagan's conservative beliefs, charm, and optimism convinced Americans that he would usher in a new era of prosperity and patriotism.

Review Questions

1. What events contributed to the rise of conservatism?

_____

_____

2. What did the Moral Majority dislike?

_____

_____

READING CHECK

What is the term for programs that the federal government requires but does not pay for?

_____

_____

_____

VOCABULARY STRATEGY

What does the word *degeneration* mean in the underlined sentence? Circle the word below that is a synonym for *degeneration.*

• advancement

• decline

READING SKILL

Summarize Describe the differences between the liberal and conservative viewpoints of government.

_____

_____

_____

Note Taking Study Guide

CHAPTER 23 SECTION 2

THE REAGAN REVOLUTION

Focus Question: What were the major characteristics of the conservative Reagan Revolution?

Identify the main ideas behind Reagan's policies.

Reagan Era		
Reaganomics	**Conservative Strength**	**Challenging Issues**
•	•	•
•	•	•
•		•
		•
		•
		•
		•
		•

CHAPTER **23** SECTION 2	**Section Summary**
	THE REAGAN REVOLUTION

President Reagan's economic policies, or "Reaganomics," were based on the theory of **supply-side economics,** which assumes that reducing taxes gives people more incentive to work and more money to spend, causing the economy to grow. The government would then collect more tax dollars without raising taxes. Congress passed the Economic Recovery Act of 1981, which reduced taxes by 25 percent over three years.

Reagan called for **deregulation,** or the removal of government control over industries, including airline and telecommunications industries. He also appointed conservative judges to federal courts.

The economy experienced a severe recession from 1980 through 1982 but rebounded in 1983. Inflation fell and the Gross National Product increased. Still, the number of poor increased and the richest grew even richer. Reagan increased defense spending but failed to win cuts in other areas of the budget, leading to a **budget deficit,** a shortfall between money spent and money collected by the government. The **national debt,** the amount of money the government owes to owners of government bonds, also rose. Deficit problems worsened when the government had to bail out depositors of the nearly 1,000 Savings and Loan banks that failed in the **Savings and Loan (S&L) crisis** of 1989.

Reagan faced other problems. American students were scoring lower on standardized tests, prompting conservatives to further lobby for **vouchers,** or government checks that could be used by parents to pay tuition at private schools. The nation also faced a new disease—**Acquired Immunodeficiency Syndrome (AIDS).** By the end of the 1980s, AIDS was the biggest killer of men between the ages of 20 and 40.

Despite these problems, Reagan remained popular and was overwhelmingly reelected in 1984. <u>However, his momentum did not lead to a triumph for conservatives in Congress.</u> Democrats retained control of the House of Representatives.

Review Questions

1. What occurred in the economy during the early 1980s?

_____

_____

2. What was the budget deficit, and what event made it worse?

_____

_____

READING CHECK

What disease became the biggest killer of men between the ages of 20 and 40 by the late 1980s?

_____

_____

_____

VOCABULARY STRATEGY

What does the word *momentum* mean in the underlined sentence? Circle any words or phrases in the paragraph that help you figure out what *momentum* means.

_____

_____

_____

READING SKILL

Identify Main Ideas Describe the central idea of Reagan's economic policies.

_____

_____

_____

Name _____ Class _____ Date _____

Focus Question: What were Reagan's foreign policies, and how did they contribute to the fall of communism in Europe?

A. *As you read this section, use the flowchart below to sequence major events related to the fall of communism in Europe and the Soviet Union.*

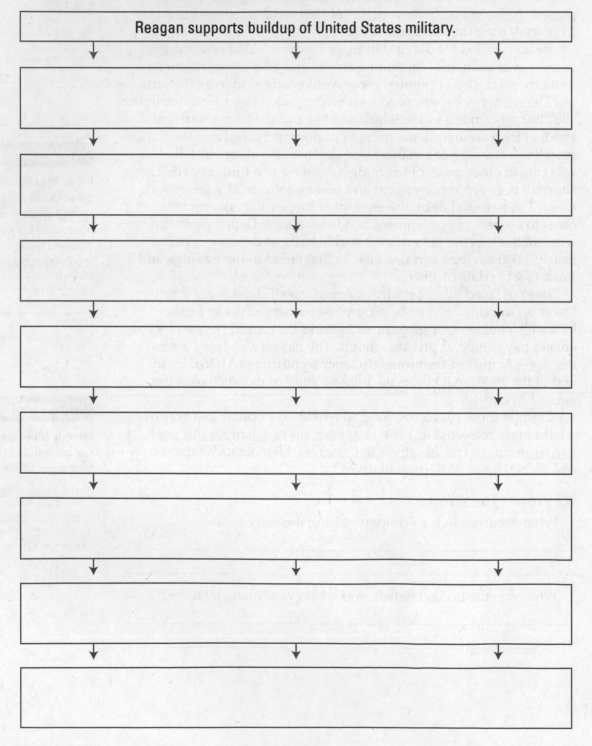

Reagan supports buildup of United States military.

CHAPTER 23 SECTION 3

Note Taking Study Guide

THE END OF THE COLD WAR

Focus Question: What were Reagan's foreign policies, and how did they contribute to the fall of communism in Europe?

B. *Record the main ideas related to events in the Middle East during Reagan's presidency in the concept web below.*

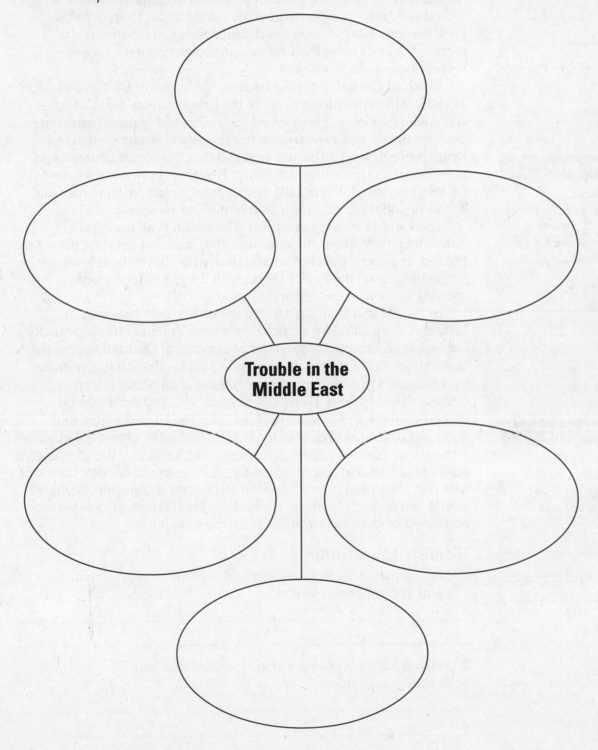

Name _____ Class _____ Date _____

READING CHECK

What country released American hostages early in Reagan's presidency?

_____

_____

_____

Under President Reagan, the United States worked to weaken communism and the Soviet Union by committing to the largest peacetime military buildup in its history. Reagan believed that the Soviet Union would be unable to match U.S. defense spending. Reagan also proposed the **Strategic Defense Initiative (SDI),** which would use lasers to destroy missiles aimed at the United States. Furthermore, Reagan supported anticommunist rebellions worldwide, including the **Contras,** anticommunist counter-revolutionaries in Nicaragua.

Mikhail Gorbachev, who became the leader of the Soviet Union in 1985, initiated reforms to move the country away from a state-controlled economy. He pursued the policies of *glasnost,* meaning a new openness, and *perestroika,* reforming the Soviet system. As Reagan predicted, Gorbachev realized that the Soviet Union could not match the U.S. military buildup. Relations between the two nations improved. Eventually both signed a nuclear arms pact and began negotiating for a reduction of nuclear weapons.

The Cold War came to an end. The Berlin Wall tumbled in November 1989. From 1989 through 1991, communists lost power in Poland, Hungary, Czechoslovakia, Bulgaria, Romania, Albania, and Yugoslavia. And the Soviet Union split into 15 independent republics when communism collapsed in 1991.

VOCABULARY STRATEGY

What does the word *contradicting* mean in the underlined sentence? Use context clues to help you figure out the meaning of *contradicting.*

_____

_____

_____

In the Middle East, 241 United States Marines stationed in Lebanon were killed by a truck bomb. The United States repeatedly clashed with Libya, whose leader Muammar al-Qaddafi supported terrorist groups. One breakthrough in Middle East affairs, minutes into Reagan's presidency, was the release of all 52 American hostages held by Iran. However, Reagan's second term was tarnished by the **Iran-Contra affair.** In 1985, the United States sold weapons to Iran in exchange for Iran's promise to pressure Lebanese terrorists to release American hostages, contradicting the administration's policy of refusing to negotiate with terrorists. Money from this sale was then used to fund Contras in Nicaragua, despite a congressional ban on such funding. Ultimately, several top officials were convicted of charges stemming from the scandal.

READING SKILL

Sequence Describe Mikhail Gorbachev's policies that brought reform to the Soviet Union prior to the collapse of communism.

_____

_____

_____

Review Questions

1. Describe the actions President Reagan took to weaken communism and the Soviet Union.

_____

_____

2. Why did the Iran-Contra affair tarnish President Reagan's presidency?

_____

_____

CHAPTER
23
SECTION 4

Note Taking Study Guide

FOREIGN POLICY AFTER THE COLD WAR

Focus Question: What actions did the United States take abroad during George H.W. Bush's presidency?

Use the chart below to summarize Bush's major foreign policy decisions.

Post-Cold War Foreign Policy	
America's new role in the world	**Persian Gulf War**
•	•
•	
	•
•	•
•	
•	

CHAPTER 23 SECTION 4

Section Summary

FOREIGN POLICY AFTER THE COLD WAR

READING CHECK

What was the name of the oppressive system of segregation in South Africa that was dismantled in the early 1990s?

_____

_____

_____

Under President George H.W. Bush, the United States took a leading role in world affairs. Bush continued the war on drugs, and in December 1989, U.S. troops invaded Panama and arrested its dictator, **Manuel Noriega.** Noriega was convicted of drug trafficking and sentenced to 40 years in an American prison.

In the spring of 1989, Chinese students staged pro-democracy protests in Beijing's **Tiananmen Square.** Americans hoped that communism might fall in China. Instead, China crushed the protest and jailed many of the activists. President Bush condemned these actions and suspended arms sales to China but retained economic and diplomatic ties.

In the early 1990s, the oppressive South African system of segregation called **apartheid** ended, in part because of American economic sanctions. Many American firms **divested,** or withdrew investments, from South Africa. **Nelson Mandela,** the previously imprisoned leader of the antiapartheid movement, was elected leader of South Africa in 1994.

VOCABULARY STRATEGY

What does the word *tolerate* mean in the underlined sentence? The word *forbid* is an antonym of *tolerate.* Use the meaning of *forbid* to help you figure out the meaning of *tolerate.*

_____

_____

_____

In the former Soviet Union, Yugoslavia was fighting a bloody civil war. Bush chose not to intervene with troops. However, later he did send United States Marines to Somalia on a humanitarian mission called "Operation Restore Hope."

Iraq's invasion of Kuwait in August 1990 was one of Bush's greatest foreign policy challenges. **Saddam Hussein,** Iraq's dictator, sought to control Kuwait's rich oil deposits and increase his power in the region.

President Bush made it clear that he would not tolerate Iraq's aggression against its neighbor. He worked to build an international coalition and backed a United Nations resolution demanding that Iraqi troops withdraw. Hussein did not comply. Under the name **Operation Desert Storm,** American, British, French, Egyptian, and Saudi coalition forces attacked Iraqi troops on January 16, 1991. On February 23, coalition forces stormed Kuwait, and within five days, Iraq agreed to a UN cease-fire. In accordance with the UN resolution, Iraqis left Kuwait, but Saddam Hussein still ruled Iraq. The entire conflict later became known as the Persian Gulf War.

READING SKILL

Summarize Summarize President Bush's approach to the Gulf War.

_____

_____

_____

Review Questions

1. Why did President Bush send troops to Panama?

_____

_____

2. Describe non-military actions Bush took to help resolve world conflicts during his presidency.

_____

_____

Note Taking Study Guide
THE COMPUTER AND TECHNOLOGY REVOLUTIONS

Focus Question: How have technological changes and globalization transformed the American economy?

As you read, fill in the flowchart below to help you categorize technological changes and their impact.

Technology Revolution		
Computers	**Communications**	**Globalization**
•	•	•
•	•	•
•	•	•
•	•	
•	•	

Name _____ Class _____ Date _____

READING CHECK

What is globalization?

_____

_____

_____

VOCABULARY STRATEGY

What does the word *access* mean in the underlined sentence? Circle any words or phrases in the surrounding sentences that help you figure out what *access* means.

_____

_____

_____

READING SKILL

Categorize Which technological change discussed in this section has had the greatest effect on the American economy? Explain.

_____

_____

_____

The rapid pace of technological change in the twentieth century touched every aspect of modern life. One of the most important innovations was the computer. The first modern computer was developed in 1946 and filled an entire basement. As technology improved, small computers called personal computers were introduced. By the 1980s, **personal computers** were transforming American business and industry. They changed medical science as well and helped create a new field called **biotechnology,** in which technology is used to solve problems affecting living organisms.

The late twentieth century ushered in the "information age." **Satellites** orbiting Earth increased the speed of global communications. Cellular telephones using satellite technology enabled people to communicate away from their homes. By the 1990s, the **Internet** made communication and access to information almost instantaneous, which in turn profoundly altered commerce, education, research, and entertainment.

These technological changes influenced how and where people worked. Fewer Americans worked in factories or on farms. Instead, they provided services. Satellites and computers increased **globalization,** the process by which national economies, politics, cultures, and societies become integrated with those of other nations around the world. A **multinational corporation** might have its financial headquarters in one country and manufacturing plants in several other countries. It might get raw materials from many different places and sell its products to a worldwide market.

Some economists say that the United States now has a **service economy.** Jobs in the service sector vary widely, from some of the highest paying, such as lawyers, to some of the lowest paying, such as fast-food workers. With the rise of the service economy and the decline of industries such as mining and manufacturing, the political power of labor unions has decreased and the average wages of workers have fallen.

Review Questions

1. How have recent developments in communications affected the way people live today?

_____

_____

2. How has the rise of the service sector affected the American economy?

_____

_____

CHAPTER 24 SECTION 2

Note Taking Study Guide
THE CLINTON PRESIDENCY

Focus Question: What were the successes and failures of the Clinton presidency?

Complete the outline below as you read to summarize information about the Clinton presidency.

I. The 1992 Election

　　A. Bush's popularity plummets.

　　B. Clinton runs as "New Democrat."

　　C. Clinton carries the election.

II. Clinton's Domestic Policies

　　A. _____

　　B. _____

　　C. _____

III. _____

　　A. _____

　　B. _____

　　C. _____

　　D. _____

IV. _____

　　A. _____

　　B. _____

　　C. _____

　　D. _____

CHAPTER 24 SECTION 2

Section Summary

THE CLINTON PRESIDENCY

Twelve years after the Reagan Revolution, Americans were ready for a change in the White House. The Democrats nominated **William Jefferson Clinton,** governor of Arkansas, to run against President Bush in the 1992 election. Texas billionaire **H. Ross Perot** ran as an independent. Clinton carried the election, and Democrats retained control of both houses of Congress.

Early in his presidency, Clinton focused on domestic issues. He signed the **Family Medical Leave Act,** which guaranteed most full-time employees unpaid leave each year for personal or family medical reasons. Clinton also oversaw passage of the **Brady Bill,** which placed a five-day waiting period on sales of handguns. Another important issue for Clinton was healthcare reform. Clinton's wife, Hillary, led a task force to investigate ways to guarantee healthcare for all Americans. The committee's proposal never won congressional support and was ultimately dropped.

VOCABULARY STRATEGY

What does the word *ultimately* mean in the underlined sentence? The term *finally* is a synonym of *ultimately.* Use this synonym to help you figure out what *ultimately* means in this sentence.

_____

_____

_____

In the 1994 midterm elections, Georgia congressman **Newt Gingrich** led the opposition to Clinton. He galvanized Republicans around his **Contract With America,** a plan that attacked big government and emphasized patriotism and traditional values. Winning the votes of Americans who felt the federal government was too big, too wasteful, and too liberal, Republicans captured the House, the Senate, and most state governorships. Once in office, Republicans passed much of Gingrich's program. Two years later, Clinton was reelected by a wide margin, although Congress remained under Republican control.

President Clinton had dodged scandals from his first day in office. One concerned investments the Clintons had made. Special prosecutor **Kenneth Starr** investigated the case for seven years but failed to uncover evidence of the Clintons' guilt. In the process, however, Starr investigated the President's relationship with a White House intern. When Clinton admitted he had lied about the affair under oath, Starr recommended **impeachment** proceedings. The House of Representatives impeached Clinton on the charges of perjury and obstruction of justice. Clinton was tried and acquitted by the Senate in February 1999.

READING SKILL

Summarize What were the most significant events of Clinton's presidency?

_____

_____

_____

Review Questions

1. What bills did President Clinton sign after taking office?

_____

_____

2. What was the Contract With America?

_____

_____

Name _____ Class _____ Date _____

Note Taking Study Guide
GLOBAL POLITICS AND ECONOMICS

Focus Question: What role did the United States take on in global politics and economics following the Cold War?

Complete the flowchart below to help you identify main ideas about global politics and economics.

U.S. Global Policy

Free Trade	Foreign Intervention	Middle East
• NAFTA	•	•
•		
	•	•
•		
	•	•

Name _____ Class _____ Date _____

READING CHECK

What authority does the WTO have that GATT did not have?

_____

_____

_____

VOCABULARY STRATEGY

Find the word *intervention* in the underlined sentence. What does *intervention* mean? Circle any words in the surrounding sentences that help you figure out what *intervention* means.

_____

_____

_____

READING SKILL

Identify Main Ideas What role did the United States play in global economics during the 1990s?

_____

_____

_____

In the 1990s, the United States was the world's sole superpower, wielding influence over economic and political events worldwide. Among the issues influenced by the United States was free trade. The **European Union (EU),** which coordinates monetary and economic policies among European nations, is an example of a free trade bloc. When the EU threatened U.S. economic leadership, the United States joined with Canada and Mexico to pass the **North American Free Trade Agreement (NAFTA).** NAFTA created a free trade zone in North America.

Clinton supported NAFTA and other free trade agreements, although many Democrats didn't. In 1994, he signed the revision to the **General Agreement on Tariffs and Trade (GATT)** aimed at reducing tariffs worldwide. In 1995, he signed the accords of the **World Trade Organization (WTO),** which replaced GATT and had greater authority to negotiate agreements and settle disputes.

On the political scene, many Americans opposed military involvement in foreign affairs, but Clinton found it necessary to intervene in conflicts in Somalia and Haiti. When civil war broke out in the former Yugoslav republic of Bosnia, Bosnian Serbs attacked and murdered Muslims and Croats. This state-sanctioned mass murder became known as **ethnic cleansing.** In 1995, Clinton asked NATO to bomb Serbian strongholds. This intervention brought about a cease-fire, but violence flared in another former Yugoslavian republic. NATO troops, including U.S. troops, responded again.

The ongoing conflict between Israelis and Palestinians escalated in the 1990s. Clinton led negotiations that produced a short-lived agreement between Israeli and Palestinian leaders. That involvement in the Middle East made the United States a target of a terrorist group called **al Qaeda.** The group launched several attacks on U.S. targets at home and abroad.

Review Questions

1. What challenge did the European Union pose to the United States?

_____

_____

2. Why did Clinton encourage NATO to become involved in the Bosnian conflict?

_____

_____

CHAPTER
24
SECTION 4

Note Taking Study Guide
BUSH AND THE WAR ON TERRORISM

Focus Question: What was the impact of Bush's domestic agenda and his response to the terrorist attack against the United States?

Record the sequence of events in Bush's presidency in the flowchart below.

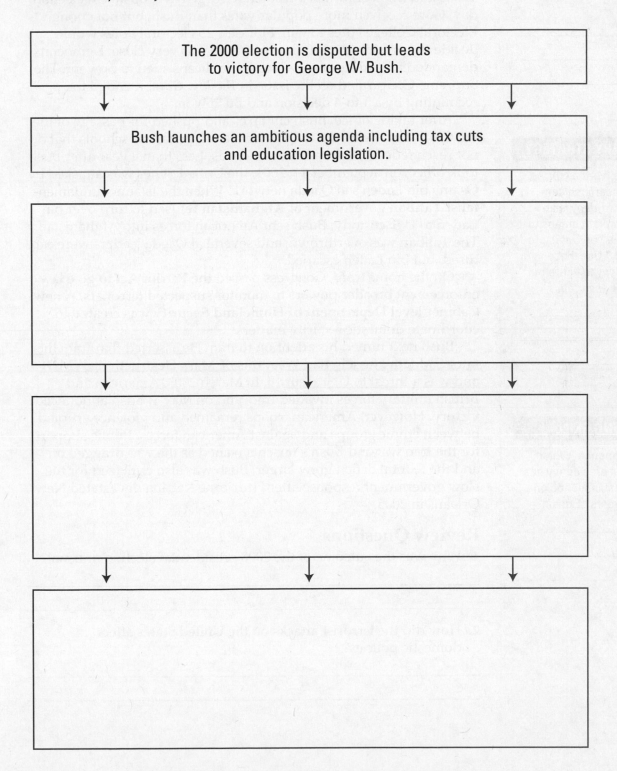

The 2000 election is disputed but leads to victory for George W. Bush.

↓   ↓   ↓

Bush launches an ambitious agenda including tax cuts and education legislation.

↓   ↓   ↓

↓   ↓   ↓

↓   ↓   ↓

CHAPTER 24 SECTION 4

Section Summary

BUSH AND THE WAR ON TERRORISM

READING CHECK

What problems did President Bush face at home following the invasion of Iraq?

_____

_____

_____

VOCABULARY STRATEGY

What does the word *asserted* mean in the underlined sentence? The word *deny* is an antonym of *assert*. It means to "declare untrue" or "refuse to accept as true." Use these meanings of *deny* to figure out the meaning of *asserted*.

_____

_____

_____

READING SKILL

Recognize Sequence Which event in Bush's presidency has had the greatest influence on subsequent events? Explain.

_____

_____

_____

Clinton's Vice President, Al Gore, Jr., was the Democratic candidate for President in 2000. He faced Green Party candidate Ralph Nader and Republican **George W. Bush.** Bush was a former governor of Texas and a son of former President George H.W. Bush. On election day, Gore received more popular votes than Bush, but not enough Electoral College votes to win. Florida's 25 electoral votes would decide the presidency, but the vote there was very close. Democrats demanded a hand recount, which Republicans sued to prevent. The Supreme Court ruled on the issue in *Bush* v. *Gore.* It ended the recounting by a 5-to-4 decision and Bush won.

After taking office, Bush cut taxes and pushed for passage of the **No Child Left Behind Act.** This legislation penalizes schools that do not reach federal performance standards. Less than a year after Bush took office, on September 11, 2001, the United States was attacked by Osama bin Laden's al Qaeda network. When the Islamic fundamentalist **Taliban** government of **Afghanistan** refused to turn over bin Laden to U.S. custody, Bush sent American forces into Afghanistan. The Taliban was overthrown, and several al Qaeda leaders were captured, but bin Laden escaped.

On the home front, Congress passed the **Patriot Act** to give law enforcement broader powers to monitor suspected terrorists. A new Cabinet-level **Department of Homeland Security** was created to coordinate domestic security matters.

Bush next turned his attention to Iraq. He asserted that Iraqi dictator Saddam Hussein had **Weapons of Mass Destruction (WMD) and was a threat to U.S. security.** In March 2003, American and British military forces invaded Iraq, and on May 1, Bush announced victory. However, American troops remained and violence erupted between ethnic groups and against American forces. Public support for the Iraq war and Bush's tax cuts waned as the war dragged on and the federal deficit grew larger. Bush was also criticized for the slow government response after Hurricane Katrina devastated New Orleans in 2005.

Review Questions

1. Why was the outcome of the 2000 presidential election unusual?

_____

_____

2. How did the terrorist attacks on the United States affect domestic policies?

_____

_____

CHAPTER
24
SECTION 5

Note Taking Study Guide
AMERICANS LOOK TO THE FUTURE

Focus Question: How was American society changing at the beginning of the twenty-first century?

Record supporting details about the changing American society in the table below.

A Changing Society	
Immigration	**Demographics**
• Immigration policies relax. • •	• Family structures change. • •

Section Summary

AMERICANS LOOK TO THE FUTURE

What is the purpose of affirmative action?

_____

_____

_____

What does the word *discrimination* mean in the underlined sentence? Use context clues to help you figure out the meaning of *discrimination*.

_____

_____

_____

Identify Supporting Details
What law increased resources to prosecute men guilty of violence against women?

_____

_____

_____

As the twenty-first century dawned, American society looked very different than it had a hundred years before. The **Immigration Act of 1990** had increased quotas by 40 percent and eased most restrictions. Since then, almost one million immigrants arrived in the United States each year. Most of the new immigrants were Latinos. They have had a profound social, cultural, and political impact. Asians make up the second-largest source of the new immigration.

Some people worry that immigrants take jobs and social services away from native-born Americans. They oppose **bilingual education,** in which students are taught in their native languages as well as in English. Proponents of immigration argue that immigrants contribute to the economy and help the nation maintain its population. Much of the debate concerns illegal immigrants. The **Immigration and Control Act of 1986** aimed to stop the flow of illegal immigrants by penalizing businesses that hired them, but illegal immigrants still regularly cross U.S. borders.

American demographics have changed, with many people moving from the Midwest and Northeast to the Sunbelt. The American family changed as well. Divorces and single-parent households are now more common than just 40 years ago.

Affirmative action was created in the 1960s to help minorities and women overcome past discrimination by giving them preference in school admissions and job applications. Today, such programs are being challenged and in some cases, ended. Even so, women and African Americans continue to make social and political gains. More African Americans now earn middle-class incomes and hold college degrees. Women are protected against unfair treatment in the workplace. The 1994 **Violence Against Women Act** increased federal resources to apprehend and prosecute men guilty of violent acts against women.

As the baby boom generation reaches retirement, falling birthrates mean there may not be enough workers to pay for their Social Security benefits. President Bush proposed **privatizing** Social Security. This change would allow younger workers to invest some of their earnings in individual retirement accounts. Opponents defeated his proposal and the debate continues.

Review Questions

1. What led to a dramatic increase in immigration to the United States at the end of the twentieth century?

_____

_____

2. How have American demographics changed in recent decades?

_____

_____

American Issues Study Guide

Global Interdependence

Enduring Question: Is global interdependence good for the American economy?

Record information about the events listed below, as you study them in your textbook.
* *Describe the situation that brought the issue into discussion.*
* *Identify the arguments at the time on both sides of the issue. Discuss the arguments for global interdependence. Then, discuss the arguments against global interdependence.*
* *Indicate how the issue was resolved at the time. Did the situation change? If so, how?*

1500s: Columbian Exchange (See chapter "The Nation's Beginnings")

_____
_____
_____
_____
_____
_____
_____

1812: War of 1812 (See chapter "The Nation's Beginnings")

_____
_____
_____
_____
_____
_____
_____

1944: World Bank (See chapter "World War II")

_____
_____
_____
_____
_____
_____
_____

American Issues Study Guide

Global Interdependence *(continued)*

1990s: World Trade Increases (See chapter "Into a New Century")

_____
_____
_____
_____
_____
_____
_____

2000s: Globalization Debated (See chapter "Into a New Century")

_____
_____
_____
_____
_____
_____
_____

Other examples in American history

_____
_____
_____
_____
_____
_____
_____
_____
_____

American Issues Study Guide

Expanding and Protecting Civil Rights

Enduring Question: What should the federal government do to expand and protect civil rights?

Record information about the events listed below, as you study them in your textbook.
* *Describe the situation that brought the issue into discussion.*
* *Identify the arguments at the time on both sides of the issue. Discuss the arguments for the government expanding rights. Then, discuss the arguments against the government expanding rights.*
* *Indicate how the issue was resolved at the time. Did the situation change? If so, how?*

1791: Bill of Rights (See chapter "The Nation's Beginnings")

_____

_____

_____

_____

_____

_____

1868: Fourteenth Amendment (See chapter "Crisis, Civil War, and Reconstruction")

_____

_____

_____

_____

_____

_____

1920: Nineteenth Amendment (See chapter "The Progressive Era")

_____

_____

_____

_____

_____

_____

American Issues Study Guide

Expanding and Protecting Civil Rights *(continued)*

1964: Civil Rights Act (See chapter "The Civil Rights Movement")

_____

_____

_____

_____

_____

_____

_____

Other examples in American history

_____

_____

_____

_____

_____

_____

_____

_____

_____

_____

_____

American Issues Study Guide

Sectionalism and National Politics

Enduring Question: How do regional differences affect national politics?

Record information about the events listed below, as you study them in your textbook.
- *Describe the situation that brought the issue into discussion.*
- *Identify the arguments at the time on both sides of the issue. Discuss the arguments for basing politics on regional differences. Then, discuss the arguments for basing politics on national interests.*
- *Indicate how the issue was resolved at the time. Did the situation change? If so, how?*

1787: Three-fifths Compromise (See chapter "The Nation's Beginnings")

_____

_____

_____

_____

_____

_____

_____

1812: War of 1812 (See chapter "The Nation's Beginnings")

_____

_____

_____

_____

_____

_____

_____

1816–1832: Tariffs (See chapter "Growth and Reform")

_____

_____

_____

_____

_____

_____

_____

Name _____ Class _____ Date _____

American Issues Study Guide

Sectionalism and National Politics *(continued)*

1861: Civil War (See chapter "Crisis, Civil War, and Reconstruction")

_____

_____

_____

_____

_____

_____

2004: Presidential Election (See chapter "Into a New Century")

_____

_____

_____

_____

_____

_____

_____

_____

Other examples in American history

_____

_____

_____

_____

_____

_____

_____

_____

_____

American Issues Study Guide

Church and State

Enduring Question: What is the proper relationship between government and religion?

Record information about the events listed below, as you study them in your textbook.
* *Describe the situation that brought the issue into discussion.*
* *Identify the arguments at the time on both sides of the issue. Discuss the arguments for separating government and religion. Then, discuss the arguments against separating government and religion.*
* *Indicate how the issue was resolved at the time. Did the situation change? If so, how?*

1791: Bill of Rights (See chapter "The Nation's Beginnings")

_____
_____
_____
_____
_____
_____
_____
_____

1840s: Sabbatarian Controversy (See chapter "Growth and Reform")

_____
_____
_____
_____
_____
_____
_____

1984: Federal Equal Access Act (See chapter "The Conservative Resurgence")

_____
_____
_____
_____
_____
_____
_____
_____

American Issues Study Guide

Church and State *(continued)*

2000: *Mitchell* v. *Helms* (See appendix "Supreme Court Cases")

_____

_____

_____

_____

_____

_____

Other examples in American history

_____

_____

_____

_____

_____

_____

_____

_____

_____

_____

American Issues Study Guide

Federal Power and States' Rights

Enduring Question: How much power should the federal government have?

Record information about the events listed below, as you study them in your textbook.
- *Describe the situation that brought the issue into discussion.*
- *Identify the arguments at the time on both sides of the issue. Describe the arguments for federal power. Then, describe the arguments for states' rights.*
- *Indicate how the issue was resolved at the time. Did the situation change? If so, how?*

1791: Bill of Rights (See chapter "The Nation's Beginnings")

_____

_____

_____

_____

_____

_____

_____

1831: Nullification Crisis (See chapter "Growth and Reform")

_____

_____

_____

_____

_____

_____

_____

1857: *Dred Scott* v. *Sandford* (See chapter "Crisis, Civil War, and Reconstruction")

_____

_____

_____

_____

_____

_____

_____

American Issues Study Guide

Federal Power and States' Rights *(continued)*

1930s: New Deal (See chapter "The New Deal")

_____
_____
_____
_____
_____
_____
_____

1965: Voting Rights Act (See chapter "The Civil Rights Movement")

_____
_____
_____
_____
_____
_____
_____

Other examples in American history

_____
_____
_____
_____
_____
_____
_____
_____
_____
_____

American Issues Study Guide

Checks and Balances

Enduring Question: Does any branch of the federal government have too much power?

Record information about the events listed below, as you study them in your textbook.
- *Describe the situation that brought the issue into discussion.*
- *Identify the arguments at the time on both sides of the issue. Discuss the arguments for balancing federal power. Then, discuss the arguments for giving one branch of the federal government more power than another.*
- *Indicate how the issue was resolved at the time. Did the situation change? If so, how?*

1803: *Marbury v. Madison* (See chapter "The Nation's Beginnings")

_____
_____
_____
_____
_____
_____
_____

1830s: Jackson Presidency (See chapter "Growth and Reform")

_____
_____
_____
_____
_____
_____
_____

1868: Johnson Impeachment (See chapter "Crisis, Civil War, and Reconstruction")

_____
_____
_____
_____
_____
_____
_____

American Issues Study Guide

Checks and Balances *(continued)*

1930s: New Deal (See chapter "The New Deal")

_____

_____

_____

_____

_____

_____

_____

1960s: Warren Court (See chapter "The Kennedy and Johnson Years")

_____

_____

_____

_____

_____

_____

_____

1973: War Powers Act (See chapter "The Vietnam War Era")

_____

_____

_____

_____

_____

_____

_____

American Issues Study Guide

2000s: War on Terrorism (See chapter "Into a New Century")

_____

_____

_____

_____

_____

_____

_____

Other examples in American history

_____

_____

_____

_____

_____

_____

_____

_____

_____

_____

American Issues Study Guide

Technology and Society

Enduring Question: What are the benefits and costs of technology?

Record information about the events listed below, as you study them in your textbook.
- *Describe the situation that brought the issue into discussion.*
- *Identify the arguments at the time on both sides of the issue. Describe the arguments in favor of new technology. Then, describe the arguments against new technology.*
- *Indicate how the issue was resolved at the time. Did the situation change? If so, how?*

Late 1700s: Factory System (See chapter "The Nation's Beginnings")

_____
_____
_____
_____
_____
_____
_____

1859: Oil Refining (See chapter "The Triumph of Industry")

_____
_____
_____
_____
_____
_____
_____

1946: Computers (See chapter "Into a New Century")

_____
_____
_____
_____
_____
_____
_____

American Issues Study Guide

1950s: Home Appliances (See chapter "Postwar Confidence and Anxiety")

_____
_____
_____
_____
_____
_____
_____

1980s: Internet (See chapter "Into a New Century")

_____
_____
_____
_____
_____
_____
_____
_____

Other examples in American history

_____
_____
_____
_____
_____
_____
_____
_____

American Issues Study Guide

Migration and Urbanization

Enduring Question: How does migration affect patterns of settlement in America?

Record information about the events listed below, as you study them in your textbook.
- *Describe the situation that brought the issue into discussion.*
- *Identify the arguments at the time on both sides of the issue. Describe the arguments in favor of migration. Describe the arguments against migration.*
- *Indicate how the issue was resolved at the time. Did the situation change? If so, how?*

1862: Homestead Act (See chapter "Immigration and Urbanization")

_____
_____
_____
_____
_____
_____
_____
_____

1880–1920: Urban Migration (See chapter "Immigration and Urbanization")

_____
_____
_____
_____
_____
_____
_____

1910–1930: Great Migration (See chapter "The Twenties")

_____
_____
_____
_____
_____
_____
_____

Name _____ Class _____ Date _____

American Issues Study Guide

1950s: Suburban Flight (See chapter "Postwar Confidence and Anxiety")

_____
_____
_____
_____
_____
_____
_____

1970s–Present: Sunbelt Growth (See chapter "A Crisis in Confidence")

_____
_____
_____
_____
_____
_____
_____
_____

Other examples in American history

_____
_____
_____
_____
_____
_____
_____
_____
_____
_____

American Issues Study Guide

American Indian Policy

Enduring Question: How should the federal government deal with Indian nations?

Record information about the events listed below, as you study them in your textbook.
* *Describe the situation that brought the issue into discussion.*
* *Identify the arguments at the time on both sides of the issue. Describe the arguments in favor of the federal government controlling Indian nations. Then, describe the arguments in favor of Indian nations exercising autonomy.*
* *Indicate how the issue was resolved at the time. Did the situation change? If so, how?*

1887: Dawes Act (See chapter "The South and West Transformed")

_____

_____

_____

_____

_____

_____

_____

1934: Indian Reorganization Act (See chapter "The New Deal")

_____

_____

_____

_____

_____

_____

_____

1975: Indian Self-Determination and Educational Assistance Act (See chapter "An Era of Protest and Change")

_____

_____

_____

_____

_____

_____

_____

American Issues Study Guide

Other examples in American history

_____

_____

_____

_____

_____

_____

_____

_____

_____

Name _____ Class _____ Date _____

American Issues Study Guide

Women in the Workplace

Enduring Question: Why do Americans disagree over women's rights?

Record information about the events listed below, as you study them in your textbook.
- *Describe the situation that brought the issue into discussion.*
- *Identify the arguments at the time on both sides of the issue. Describe the arguments in favor of giving women more rights. Describe the arguments against expanding rights for women.*
- *Indicate how the issue was resolved at the time. Did the situation change? If so, how?*

1848: Seneca Falls Convention (See chapter "Growth and Reform")

_____

_____

_____

_____

_____

_____

_____

1920: Nineteenth Amendment (See chapter "The Progressive Era")

_____

_____

_____

_____

_____

_____

_____

1964: Title VII of the Civil Rights Act (See chapter "An Era of Protest and Change")

_____

_____

_____

_____

_____

_____

_____

American Issues Study Guide

1972: Title IX of the Education Codes (See chapter "An Era of Protest and Change")

_____
_____
_____
_____
_____
_____
_____

Other examples in American history

_____
_____
_____
_____
_____
_____
_____
_____
_____
_____
_____

American Issues Study Guide

Social Problems and Reforms

Enduring Question: What are the most pressing problems, and how can we solve them?

Record information about the events listed below, as you study them in your textbook.
- *Describe the situation that brought the issue into discussion.*
- *Identify the arguments at the time on both sides of the issue. Discuss the arguments for social reforms. Then, discuss the arguments against social reforms.*
- *Indicate how the issue was resolved at the time. Did the situation change? If so, how?*

1790s–1820s: Second Great Awakening (See chapter "Growth and Reform")

_____

_____

_____

_____

_____

_____

_____

1830s–1850s: Abolitionism (See chapter "Growth and Reform")

_____

_____

_____

_____

_____

_____

_____

1890–1920: Progressivism (See chapter "The Progressive Era")

_____

_____

_____

_____

_____

_____

_____

American Issues Study Guide

1950s–1960s: Civil Rights (See chapter "The Civil Rights Movement")

_____

_____

_____

_____

_____

_____

1990s–2000s: Healthcare Reform (See chapter "Into a New Century")

_____

_____

_____

_____

_____

_____

_____

Other examples in American history

_____

_____

_____

_____

_____

_____

_____

_____

American Issues Study Guide

Territorial Expansion of the United States

Enduring Question: Should the United States expand its territory?

Record information about the events listed below, as you study them in your textbook.
* *Describe the situation that brought the issue into discussion.*
* *Identify the arguments at the time on both sides of the issue. Discuss the arguments for territorial expansion. Then, discuss the arguments against territorial expansion.*
* *Indicate how the issue was resolved at the time. Did the situation change? If so, how?*

1803: Louisiana Purchase (See chapter "The Nation's Beginnings")

_____
_____
_____
_____
_____
_____
_____

1845: Texas Annexation (See chapter "Growth and Reform")

_____
_____
_____
_____
_____
_____
_____

1848: Mexican Cession (See chapter "Growth and Reform")

_____
_____
_____
_____
_____
_____
_____

Name _____ Class _____ Date _____

American Issues Study Guide

1867: Alaska Purchase (See chapter "An Emerging World Power")

_____

_____

_____

_____

_____

1893: Hawaiian Revolt (See chapter "An Emerging World Power")

_____

_____

_____

_____

_____

_____

_____

1898: Spanish-American War (See chapter "An Emerging World Power")

_____

_____

_____

_____

_____

_____

Other examples in American history

_____

_____

_____

_____

_____

_____

_____

Name _____ Class _____ Date _____

American Issues Study Guide

America Goes to War

Enduring Question: When should America go to war?

Record information about the events listed below, as you study them in your textbook.
* *Describe the situation that brought the issue into discussion.*
* *Identify the arguments at the time on both sides of the issue. Discuss the arguments in favor of going to war. Then, describe the arguments against going to war.*
* *Indicate how the issue was resolved at the time. Did the situation change? If so, how?*

1812: War of 1812 (See chapter "The Nation's Beginnings")

_____

_____

_____

_____

_____

_____

_____

1860s: Civil War (See chapter "Crisis, Civil War, and Reconstruction")

_____

_____

_____

_____

_____

_____

_____

1917–1918: World War I (See chapter "World War I and Beyond")

_____

_____

_____

_____

_____

_____

_____

American Issues Study Guide

1940s: World War II (See chapter "World War II")

_____

_____

_____

_____

_____

_____

1960s–1970s: Vietnam War (See chapter "The Vietnam War Era")

_____

_____

_____

_____

_____

_____

_____

Other examples in American history

_____

_____

_____

_____

_____

_____

_____

_____

_____

American Issues Study Guide

U.S. Immigration Policy

Enduring Question: How should government regulate immigration?

Record information about the events listed below, as you study them in your textbook.
* *Describe the situation that brought the issue into discussion.*
* *Identify the arguments at the time on both sides of the issue. Discuss the arguments in favor of immigration. Then, discuss the arguments against immigration.*
* *Indicate how the issue was resolved at the time. Did the situation change? If so, how?*

1882: Chinese Exclusion Act (See chapter "Immigration and Urbanization")

_____

_____

_____

_____

_____

_____

_____

_____

1924: National Origins Act (See chapter "The Twenties")

_____

_____

_____

_____

_____

_____

_____

_____

1965: Immigration Act Amended (See chapter "The Kennedy and Johnson Years")

_____

_____

_____

_____

_____

_____

_____

American Issues Study Guide

1986: Immigration Reform and Control Act (See chapter "Into a New Century")

_____

_____

_____

_____

_____

_____

_____

Other examples in American history

_____

_____

_____

_____

_____

_____

_____

_____

_____

_____

_____

American Issues Study Guide

Government's Role in the Economy

Enduring Question: What is the proper balance between free enterprise and government regulation of the economy?

Record information about the events listed below, as you study them in your textbook.
* *Describe the situation that brought the issue into discussion.*
* *Identify the arguments at the time on both sides of the issue. Describe the arguments in favor of free enterprise. Describe the arguments in favor of government regulation of the economy.*
* *Indicate how the issue was resolved at the time. Did the situation change? If so, how?*

1890: Sherman Antitrust Act (See chapter "Immigration and Urbanization")

_____
_____
_____
_____
_____
_____
_____

1906: Pure Food and Drug Act (See chapter "The Progressive Era")

_____
_____
_____
_____
_____
_____
_____

1913: Federal Reserve Act (See chapter "The Progressive Era")

_____
_____
_____
_____
_____
_____
_____

American Issues Study Guide

1933: Agricultural Adjustment Act (See chapter "The New Deal")

_____

_____

_____

_____

_____

_____

2001: Tax Cuts (See chapter "Into a New Century")

_____

_____

_____

_____

_____

_____

_____

Other examples in American history

_____

_____

_____

_____

_____

_____

_____

American Issues Study Guide

Civil Liberties and National Security

Enduring Question: What is the proper balance between national security and civil liberties?

Record information about the events listed below, as you study them in your textbook.
- *Describe the situation that brought the issue into discussion.*
- *Identify the arguments at the time on both sides of the issue. Discuss the arguments for limiting civil liberties. Discuss the arguments against limiting civil liberties.*
- *Indicate how the issue was resolved at the time. Did the situation change? If so, how?*

1790s: Undeclared War With France (See chapter "The Nation's Beginnings")

_____

_____

_____

_____

_____

_____

_____

1860s: Civil War (See chapter "Crisis, Civil War, and Reconstruction")

_____

_____

_____

_____

_____

_____

_____

1940s: World War II (See chapter "World War II")

_____

_____

_____

_____

_____

_____

_____

American Issues Study Guide

1950s: Cold War (See chapter "The Cold War")

_____

_____

_____

_____

_____

_____

_____

2001: War on Terrorism (See chapter "Into a New Century")

_____

_____

_____

_____

_____

_____

_____

_____

Other examples in American history

_____

_____

_____

_____

_____

_____

_____

_____

_____

American Issues Study Guide

Voting Rights

Enduring Question: What should the government do to promote voting rights?

Record information about the events listed below, as you study them in your textbook.
* *Describe the situation that brought the issue into discussion.*
* *Identify the arguments at the time on both sides of the issue. Describe the arguments in favor of full electoral rights. Describe the arguments in favor of limited electoral rights.*
* *Indicate how the issue was resolved at the time. Did the situation change? If so, how?*

1820s–1830s: Age of Jackson (See chapter "Growth and Reform")

_____
_____
_____
_____
_____
_____
_____

1870: Fifteenth Amendment (See chapter "Crisis, Civil War, and Reconstruction")

_____
_____
_____
_____
_____
_____
_____

1920: Nineteenth Amendment (See chapter "The Progressive Era")

_____
_____
_____
_____
_____
_____
_____

American Issues Study Guide

1965: Voting Rights Act (See chapter "The Civil Rights Movement")

_____

_____

_____

_____

_____

_____

1971: Twenty-sixth Amendment (See appendix "Constitution")

_____

_____

_____

_____

_____

_____

_____

2000: Presidential Election (See chapter "Into a New Century")

_____

_____

_____

_____

_____

_____

Other examples in American history

_____

_____

_____

_____

_____

_____

Name _____ Class _____ Date _____

American Issues Study Guide

Poverty and Prosperity

Enduring Question: How should Americans deal with the gap between rich and poor?

Record information about the events listed below, as you study them in your textbook.
- *Describe the situation that brought the issue into discussion.*
- *Identify the arguments at the time on both sides of the issue. Discuss the arguments for government policies to distribute wealth. Discuss the arguments for private help for the poor.*
- *Indicate how the issue was resolved at the time. Did the situation change? If so, how?*

1933: New Deal (See chapter "The New Deal")

_____
_____
_____
_____
_____
_____
_____

1964: War on Poverty (See chapter "The Kennedy and Johnson Years")

_____
_____
_____
_____
_____
_____

1980s: Reaganomics (See chapter "The Conservative Resurgence")

_____
_____
_____
_____
_____
_____
_____

American Issues Study Guide

1996: Welfare Reform (See chapter "Into a New Century")

_____

_____

_____

_____

_____

_____

_____

Other examples in American history

_____

_____

_____

_____

_____

_____

_____

_____

_____

_____

_____

Name _____ Class _____ Date _____

America and the World

Enduring Question: What is America's role in the world?

Record information about the events listed below, as you study them in your textbook.
* *Describe the situation that brought the issue into discussion.*
* *Identify the arguments at the time on both sides of the issue. Describe the arguments in favor of America playing an active part in world affairs. Then, describe the arguments against America getting involved in other countries' affairs.*
* *Indicate how the issue was resolved at the time. Did the situation change? If so, how?*

1823: Monroe Doctrine (See chapter "The Nation's Beginnings")

_____
_____
_____
_____
_____
_____
_____

1898: Spanish-American War (See chapter "An Emerging World Power")

_____
_____
_____
_____
_____
_____
_____

1950s–1990s: Cold War (See chapter "The Vietnam War Era")

_____
_____
_____
_____
_____
_____
_____
_____

American Issues Study Guide

2000s: War on Terrorism (See chapter "Into a New Century")

_____
_____
_____
_____
_____
_____
_____

Other examples in American history

_____
_____
_____
_____
_____
_____
_____
_____
_____
_____
_____
_____

American Issues Study Guide

Interaction With the Environment

Enduring Question: How can we balance economic development and environmental protection?

Record information about the events listed below, as you study them in your textbook.
* *Describe the situation that brought the issue into discussion.*
* *Identify the arguments at the time on both sides of the issue. Describe the arguments in favor of economic development. Then, describe the arguments in favor of environmental protection.*
* *Indicate how the issue was resolved at the time. Did the situation change? If so, how?*

1872: Yellowstone (See chapter "The Progressive Era")

_____

_____

_____

_____

_____

_____

_____

1962: *Silent Spring* (See chapter "An Era of Protest and Change")

_____

_____

_____

_____

_____

_____

1970: Clean Air Act (See chapter "An Era of Protest and Change")

_____

_____

_____

_____

_____

_____

American Issues Study Guide

1973: Endangered Species Act (See chapter "An Era of Protest and Change")

_____
_____
_____
_____
_____
_____
_____

Other examples in American history

_____
_____
_____
_____
_____
_____
_____
_____
_____
_____
_____

American Issues Study Guide

Education and American Society

Enduring Question: What should be the goals of American education?

Record information about the events listed below, as you study them in your textbook.
- *Describe the situation that brought the issue into discussion.*
- *Identify the arguments at the time on both sides of the issue. Discuss the arguments for focusing education on performance standards. Then, discuss the arguments for focusing education on democratic values.*
- *Indicate how the issue was resolved at the time. Did the situation change? If so, how?*

1903: Du Bois-Washington Debate (See chapter "The Progressive Era")

_____

_____

_____

_____

_____

_____

_____

1960: California Master Plan (See chapter "Postwar Confidence and Anxiety")

_____

_____

_____

_____

_____

_____

_____

1965: Elementary and Secondary Education Act (See chapter "The Kennedy and Johnson Years")

_____

_____

_____

_____

_____

_____

_____

American Issues Study Guide

2001: No Child Left Behind Act (See chapter "Into a New Century")

_____

_____

_____

_____

_____

_____

Other examples in American history

_____

_____

_____

_____

_____

_____

_____

_____

_____

CURRICULUM

CURRICULUM